Birds of Prey

Birds of Prey

BY DOROTHY CHILDS HOGNER

ILLUSTRATED BY NILS HOGNER

THOMAS Y. CROWELL COMPANY   NEW YORK

By the Author

BIRDS OF PREY

A BOOK OF SNAKES

BUTTERFLIES

EARTHWORMS

FROGS AND POLLIWOGS

GRASSHOPPERS AND CRICKETS

MOTHS

SNAILS

SPIDERS

WATER BEETLES

WEEDS

ACKNOWLEDGMENTS

For the loan of mounted birds and the skins of birds of prey and for answering questions, we wish to thank David H. Parsons, chief preparator of exhibits, and Mrs. Eleanor Stickney of the Peabody Museum of Natural History at Yale University; Miss Martha Sykes, Sharon (Connecticut) Audubon Center; John Mitchell, director of the Roaring Brook Nature Center, Canton, Connecticut; Miss Grace Palmer of the Philadelphia Academy of Natural Sciences, and Mr. Gordon Loery, director of the Litchfield Nature Center Museum and conservationist of the White Memorial Foundation, Litchfield, Connecticut.

For a dramatic display of his collection of living birds of prey, and for answering questions, we wish to thank Dr. Heinz Meng, ornithologist and falconer of the State University College, New Paltz, New York.

We also wish to thank our friend Dr. S. Dillon Ripley, ornithologist and secretary of the Smithsonian Institution, Washington, D.C., for checking the pictures of the birds of prey.

Dorothy Childs Hogner
Nils Hogner

CONTENTS

Introduction 1
A Forenote on Classification 8

DIURNAL BIRDS OF PREY: Vultures,
 Hawks, and Falcons 11
American Vultures 12
Hawks and Harriers 18
 Kites 18
 Short-winged Bird Hawks 26
 Broad-winged Rodent Hawks or Buteos 34
 Eagles 55
 Harriers 63
Osprey 65
Caracaras and Falcons 69
 Falconry 72
 Falcons 74

NOCTURNAL BIRDS OF PREY: Owls 87
Barn Owl 89
Typical Owls 92

PROTECTION OF BIRDS OF PREY 124
 A Unique Sanctuary: Hawk Mountain 125
 Patuxent Wildlife Research Center 127
Index 129

INTRODUCTION

Among the birds of prey are some of the biggest birds in North America—for example, the great eagles and the California Condor. Others are of medium size, and a few are small. In fact one bird of prey is no bigger in body size than a large sparrow. But all, large or small, are more or less fierce in their habits of attack.

Actually the two groups in which birds of prey are classified—the Diurnal Birds of Prey (Order *Falconiformes*), the Vultures, Hawks, and Falcons, and the Nocturnal Birds of Prey (Order *Strigiformes*), the Owls —are not closely related. It is in their habits as birds of prey that they are similar.

Birds of prey are carnivorous birds—meat eaters. Most of them hunt living mammals, such as mice, squirrels, rabbits, woodchucks, and even skunks. A number of them hunt birds, including songbirds, game birds, and water fowl. They also take frogs and other amphibians, snakes and other reptiles. A few subsist on fish.

Although the majority live mainly on the vertebrate animals such as those listed above, some include large insects in their diets.

A few species of birds of prey feed almost exclusively on carrion—the flesh of dead animals.

With the exception of the falcons, the birds of prey kill with their talons, or claws. Then they tear the meat apart with their beaks. The falcons strike with their talons, but may finish the kill with their beaks.

When devouring food, full-grown birds of prey may swallow small animals and birds whole. They tear the bigger prey into small pieces for themselves and their young. In either case, the indigestible parts are swallowed with the meat. After the digestible food has been absorbed, the stomach muscles roll the fur, feathers, and bones into pellets that the birds regurgitate before eating again.

Although a few are ugly when viewed close up, notably the vultures, most are handsome birds, and dramatic in flight. Many, such as the eagles and the Broad-winged Hawks, and the vultures, too, soar in magnificent circles. The falcons dive-bomb their prey

2

with tactics that cannot help but bring admiration from the bird watcher.

Different species of birds of prey are seen in all parts of North America, from the barren Arctic to the tropics. Some inhabit the high mountains and plateaus. Others prefer the open plains and deserts. Still others drift from forests and woody hills to the valleys, and some haunt the seaside and shores of large bodies of water, or are at home in swampy areas alongside rivers.

The birds make their nests in suitable locations within their habitat. Some build large nests, high up in tall trees, or on cliffs. Others nest in caves, in natural cavities in trees, in crevices in outbuildings, or directly on the ground. Certain desert species raise their young in holes in giant cacti.

Nest of a Marsh Hawk

Many species return to their old nests, year after year, making the nests larger and larger each year. A few use no nesting material at all. Others take over abandoned nests of crows and hawks and woodpeckers.

Most birds of prey lay only a few eggs at each nesting, two to four, or four or five. Some species mate for life, although if one mate dies, the survivor soon takes a new mate. With a few exceptions, the female does the incubating of the eggs, and the male brings food to the female when she is on the nest. The male also helps build the nest.

Both birds bring food to the young, which are voracious eaters, and the parent birds have to work hard to satisfy the fledglings' appetites, as well as their own. Often the male does most of the hunting, while the female remains near the nest.

The length of time it takes for the eggs to hatch does not vary much among the smaller and larger species of birds of prey, often about twenty-eight to thirty-four days. But in general, the young of the smaller species are ready to leave the nest much sooner than the young of the larger species. The young Red-tailed Hawk is ready to leave at six weeks of age. The fledgling Bald Eagle takes off at the age of ten to thirteen weeks. The young of the giant California Condor does not leave its nest for twenty weeks, and is dependent on its parents for longer than that.

Some birds of prey are resident within their breeding range all year around. Many, however, go south to a warmer climate in the fall of the year. Those from the Far North come south to our northern and southern states; some continue on into Mexico, while a few journey down to southern South America. The migrations are dramatic. Great flocks of hawks, ospreys, eagles, and other birds of prey wing their way over the regular flyways that they follow every year in four regions of the United States: the Atlantic, the Mississippi, the Central, and the Pacific flyways. Some birds follow the seacoast, some skirt the shores of big lakes, while many others follow mountain ridges, taking advantage of the updraft of the thermal currents to help them on their way.

Birds of prey are among the most beneficial species of wildlife, although until recently they have been lumped together by farmers and hunters as enemies of chickens and game birds. It is true that some birds of prey will take a chicken or a pigeon when living near a chicken farm or a dovecote, but only a few make up a large portion of their food on birds.

And today chicken farms may almost be discounted as a temptation to Chicken Hawks because most commercial chicken farmers now raise their poultry in confinement. Birds of prey thus have little opportunity to make nuisances of themselves as chicken thieves, except among home flocks that are allowed to range.

Many species of birds of prey do endless good on farms by taking literally millions of mice, rats, rabbits, and other nuisance mammals and insects. Mice and rats get into grain bins on farms, gnaw the bark off young fruit trees in orchards, and damage many ornamental plants in the same way. Insects damage garden and grain crops by chewing and sucking the leaves and flowers.

In the wild, birds of prey weed out ill or crippled game or other wildlife, both birds and mammals, and thus help to keep a healthy balance in nature.

Now as to what a bird of prey looks like, there are certain identifiable points. A sharply hooked bill is a common characteristic. It is used to tear the prey to pieces. In the birds of prey, either three toes are permanently pointed forward, as in the vultures, hawks, and falcons, or the outer toe may be moved at will, forward or backward, as in the owls and the osprey.

Another characteristic of birds of prey is the cere, the soft, waxlike membrane at the base of the upper bill.

For identification of species in the field, study particularly the shape of the bird's wings—whether they are rounded and broad (certain hawks), rounded and short (certain other hawks), or narrow and pointed (falcons). Also study the size and form of the bird and its characteristic way of flying.

The color of the plumage is, of course, important,

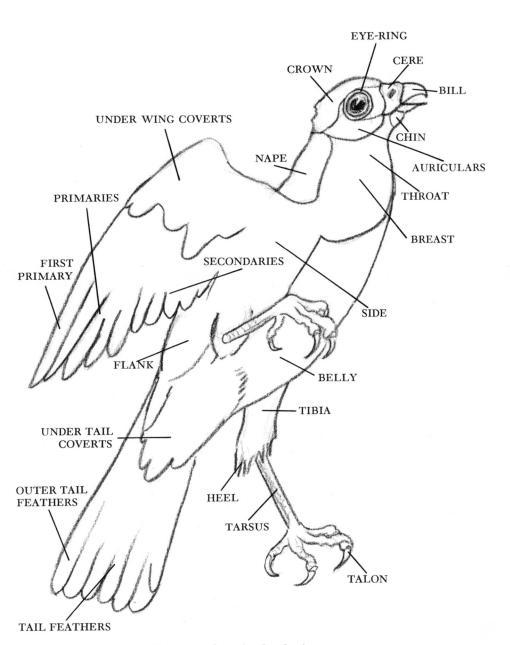

EYE-RING

CROWN

CERE

BILL

UNDER WING COVERTS

CHIN

NAPE

AURICULARS

PRIMARIES

THROAT

FIRST
PRIMARY

BREAST

SECONDARIES

SIDE

FLANK

BELLY

TIBIA

UNDER TAIL
COVERTS

OUTER TAIL
FEATHERS

HEEL

TARSUS

TALON

TAIL FEATHERS

Topography of a bird of prey

but presents difficulties among closely related species, since there is a difference in plumage between the young but fully feathered birds and the adults. The baby birds are downy, but become fully feathered before leaving the nest. The birds of prey molt, that is they change their feathers every year thereafter except in the biggest eagles and condors. The plumage of birds in their first year (juvenile) and the plumage of young birds in their second year, and with some of the bigger species in their third or fourth years (immature), is in most cases quite different in color or markings from the adult birds. A bird grows its adult feathers when it is ready to breed, although a few do breed in immature plumage.

Not only is there this difference in plumage between the young but fully feathered birds, and the adults, but there is often a darker, melanistic—black—phase, or a lighter phase, of a particular species in certain parts of the country. Albinos are seen from time to time. In other species there is also a plumage difference between the sexes.

As to size, the figures given in the text are approximate. There is variation between individuals in each species.

A FORENOTE ON CLASSIFICATION If you look up the birds of prey in one of the older, standard

Immature Cooper's Hawk

reference books, you may find yourself confused by the Latin names given in this book. The names used here are from the latest Check-list of North American Birds published by the American Ornithologists' Union. For example, Order *Falconiformes*, which includes the vultures, hawks, and falcons, was formerly Order *Raptores*. A specific example of change—the Red-tailed Hawk, now classed as *Buteo jamaicensis*, was formerly *Buteo borealis borealis*.

So when you use books published some years ago, unless you are familiar with the earlier classification, look the bird up in the index under its common name. Common names have remained fairly constant over the years.

DIURNAL BIRDS
OF PREY:
Vultures, Hawks, and Falcons

ORDER *FALCONIFORMES*

The diurnal birds of prey, as their name indicates, are with very few exceptions active only by day. Most of them, with notable exceptions, are stocky birds with wide wings. The face is not flat as that of most owls. The tibia, or upper part of the leg—and in some species also the tarsus, or lower part of the leg—is feathered. The talons are long and curved.

There are four families of diurnal birds of prey in the United States: American Vultures (Family *Cathartidae*); Hawks and Harriers (Family *Accipitridae*), subdivided into Kites, Short-winged Bird Hawks, Broad-winged Rodent Hawks, Eagles, and the Harriers; Ospreys (Family *Pandionidae*); and Caracaras and Falcons (Family *Falconidae*).

11

AMERICAN VULTURES:
Family *Cathartidae*

A vulture is at once identified by its head. The head and part of the neck are bare of feathers, and in this respect the vulture is unlike other birds of prey.

Vultures are scavengers. They have weaker claws than hawks, eagles, and falcons, and so are not well fitted for killing prey. They feed almost entirely on carrion, the flesh of dead animals. They are beneficial to man because they clean up carrion that would otherwise be a breeding place for flies and other insects that sometimes carry disease.

Vultures eat sheep and cattle that die on the range. They eat rats, rabbits, wild sheep, and other animals that die in the wild. They also feed on dead fish, frogs, and toads.

There are three species of North American vultures.

TURKEY VULTURE: Cathartes aura

Look up in the sky and see the big Turkey Vulture sail slowly, slowly, tipping its wings, and circling, circling in easy rhythm, truly floating through the air. The wingspread is six feet. The wings in flight are held in a wide V.

Then see the vulture perched, all of two and a half feet tall, with a corrugated red head and neck that are bare, save for a few bristles—a really ugly-looking and awkward bird. The contrast between the appearance of the Turkey Vulture in the air and on the ground is remarkable indeed.

Turkey Vultures live almost everywhere, flying over mountains and valleys, deserts and plains.

The Turkey Vulture is a beneficial species, since it feeds almost entirely on carrion. It has very keen eyesight and can spot dead animals from high in the sky. It does supplement its diet sometimes with living birds, frogs, toads, and insects.

These vultures roost at night, sometimes in small flocks, usually in trees. They nest on the ground under

Turkey Vulture

thorny bushes or on cliffs or in hollow stumps, without nesting material. There are one or two eggs, and the male shares in the incubation with the female.

The bare head and upper neck of the adult Turkey Vulture are reddish in color. The plumage is iridescent dark brown above, with grayish feather edgings. The underparts are brown. The bill is white, the feet pale yellowish, the eyes brown.

The young have black heads, with down.

The Turkey Vulture's range is extensive, from southern Canada throughout the United States and southward to the Strait of Magellan in South America.

BLACK VULTURE: *Coragyps atratus*

The Black Vulture closely resembles the Turkey Vulture. It may be distinguished from the Turkey Vulture—with which it sometimes associates—by its much shorter tail, by the white markings on its underwings, and by the horizontal position of its wings when sailing in flight. Flapping its wings heavily and often, it does not have the grace of flight of the Turkey Vulture. It has a length of about twenty-seven inches and a wing-spread of five feet.

The nesting and feeding habits are similar to those of the Turkey Vulture, but the Black Vulture often lives near or in cities, particularly in the tropics, where

14

it may be seen perching on rooftops. It is a very useful scavenger, particularly near slaughterhouses.

With the exception of the white underwing markings, the adult bird's coloring is black. The feathers extend in a V up the back of the head, but the rest of the head and part of the neck are bare with black, wrinkled skin. The beak is blue-gray, the eyes brown, the legs and feet gray.

The young are like the adult in plumage but have downy necks.

The Black Vulture is quite common in the warmer parts of the United States—from Arizona to southern Illinois and Indiana and east to Maryland—and south to Argentina in South America. It is seen occasionally in the Dakotas and other northern states.

CALIFORNIA CONDOR: *Gymnogyps californianus*

The California Condor is the largest bird of prey in North America. This majestic, soaring vulture has a length of from four to four and a half feet, a wingspread of nine or more feet, and weighs about twenty pounds.

The Condor also has the unfortunate distinction of being one of our rarest birds today. Shooting by man is only one of the causes of the Condor's decline in numbers. When stockmen pastured their sheep and cattle within the California Condor's range, they often set out poisoned bait in a dead animal to kill the wolves and coyotes that attacked their flocks and herds. Since Condors, like the other American vultures, feed mostly on carrion, they were poisoned.

The Condors nest on cliffs in the high mountains, and the fact that there are only one or two eggs every other year further reduces their chance to survive. The birds use no nesting materials.

When viewed perched, the California Condor is as ugly as any other vulture. The orange-colored head and neck of the adult are bare, except for a few bristles. The plumage of this great bird is dark gray-brown with white underwing coverts. The eyes are red, and the beak and legs flesh-colored.

The young have dark downy heads, and no white on their underwing coverts.

These great vultures formerly ranged over the Pacific Coast from Washington to northern Baja California. Now the forty or so remaining birds (according to a 1964 count) live in the coastal range of southern California, where they are protected by state law, with a penalty of one year in jail and a fine of from $500 to $1,000 for anyone who kills a Condor. Two sanctuaries have been established by the United States Forest Service in the Los Padres National Forest.

California Condor

HAWKS and HARRIERS:
Family *Accipitridae*

This large family is subdivided into several groups: the Kites, the Short-winged Bird Hawks, the Broad-winged Rodent Hawks and the Eagles, and the Harriers.

KITES: Subfamilies *Elaninae, Perninae,* and *Milvinae*

The kites are rather slender, graceful, swift, hawk-like birds. Most kites have long, pointed wings and deeply forked tails.

There are three subfamilies in North America: the White-tailed Kites (*Elaninae*), the Swallow-tailed Kites (*Perninae*), and the True Kites (*Milvinae*).

WHITE-TAILED KITE: *Elanus leucurus*

This now-rare kite has long, pointed wings and flies with its wing tips pointed downward. In flight it may be recognized by its long white tail and its white underwings with distinctive black patches on the underwing coverts. Its length is about seventeen inches. The wingspread is up to forty inches.

The White-tailed Kite is nonmigratory and lives within its breeding range in open and mostly marshy grasslands and on the borders of rivers, where it finds the prey it seeks—mice and other small mammals, insects, frogs, and small reptiles.

18

The White-tailed Kite makes its nest of twigs lined with grass in an oak or other deciduous tree. The female lays three to five eggs.

In general the plumage of the adult is slate-gray above and white below. Besides the distinctive features mentioned above, the adult may be recognized by its black shoulder patches. The feet and cere are orange, the eyes red, the bill black.

The young are heavily marked with brown, both above and below.

The range of the White-tailed Kite is in California

White-tailed Kite

west of the desert country, southern Texas, and from southern Florida south through eastern Mexico to British Honduras. In California it seems to be increasing in number.

SWALLOW-TAILED KITE: Elanoides forficatus

This kite is well named, for in form, and in its actions, too, it closely resembles a true swallow. It is, of course, much bigger than a swallow, being about twenty-four inches in length, a good bit of which is in the long, forked tail. The wingspread is up to fifty inches.

The Swallow-tailed Kite probably spends more time in the air than do many other birds of prey, for it often feeds in midair. The bird takes insects, such as dragonflies, on the wing, and descends to catch ground insects, small snakes and other small reptiles, and frogs, taking its prey aloft to finish the meal in the air.

The Swallow-tailed Kite flies with light airy grace, circling and soaring, dipping and turning.

These kites build their nests of twigs and Spanish moss high up in pine or cypress trees near swamps. The female lays from two to four eggs. Both sexes share in the incubation.

The adult plumage of this graceful bird is striking. The entire head and neck and underparts are snow-white. The back, wings, and tail are jet black, with some

Swallow-tailed Kite

purple and greenish luster on the lower back. The beak is black, the feet and cere pale blue, the eyes brown.

The young are quite like the adult in plumage but their breasts, heads, and necks are streaked with black, and the wing and tail feathers are white-edged.

Gone from much of its former range in North America, the Swallow-tailed Kite is accidental in southern

Canada and in our northern states from Wisconsin to New York, Pennsylvania, and New England. It is more common in the South in southern Texas, Louisiana, South Carolina, Georgia, and particularly Florida, and winters south into South America.

MISSISSIPPI KITE: *Ictinia misisippiensis*

This small, graceful kite of blue-gray plumage is almost as deft in the air as the Swallow-tailed Kite. The tail is quite long and slightly forked. The bird is about fourteen inches in length and has a wingspread of thirty-six inches.

It soars high, circles or hovers, watching for insects on the wing, or it swoops down and takes frogs, small snakes and other small reptiles on the ground.

The Mississippi Kite makes its nest of sticks in tall trees. One to three eggs are usual, and both the male and the female share in the incubation.

The front of the head of the adult is very pale bluish gray. The rest of the upperparts and the underparts are blue-gray. The tail is very dark, almost black. The bill is black, the eyes red, the feet yellow.

The underparts, head, and neck of the young are whitish, spotted with brown. There is a white stripe over each eye. The upperparts are dark brown, edged with white. The tail is black, with three slate-colored bars and white spots.

The Mississippi Kite breeds from the middle western states south through Tennessee and South Carolina into Texas and the other southern states, including northern Florida. It is accidental in New Jersey and Pennsylvania, Colorado and Nebraska. Its winter range is from southern Florida and Texas south through Mexico.

Mississippi Kite

EVERGLADE KITE or SNAIL KITE:
Rostrhamus sociabilis

These dark colored kites, which belong to the same subfamily as the Mississippi Kite, may be distinguished by their broad wings, their square, slightly notched tails, and their distinctive tail markings. They are eighteen inches in length, with a forty-four-inch wingspread.

Everglade Kites are very rare in this country today and are found only in a few large marshes in southern Florida. There they soar high over the marsh grasses, or more often fly slowly and hover low, looking for the only food they like—a large freshwater snail (*Pomacea paludosa*). When they catch a snail, they take it away to a convenient perch, where they extract the mollusk from its shell with their peculiarly adapted, slender, very hooked bill. Heaps of snail shells show where the birds have fed.

Snail Kites nest on grassy clumps, on stumps, or in bushes, in colonies. They lay two or three eggs, and both the male and the female help in the incubation.

The adult male Everglade Kite is dark bodied, slate-gray mostly, with a white tail that is crossed with a broad black band near the tip. The eyes are red, the legs and feet orange. The adult females and the young are brown above, with streakings of brown on buff underparts, and a brown band on the tail.

Though still a common species in South America,

the Everglade Kite is nearly extinct in the United States. The few remaining birds are seen in the freshwater marshes around Lake Okeechobee and in the Loxahatchee National Wildlife Refuge in Florida. The decline in numbers was brought about first by shooting and, more recently, a changing habitat. The Florida

Everglade Kite

marshes were drained for agricultural purposes and for housing developments, and drought and fires further dried up swampy areas where the kites lived.

It is also thought that a liver fluke, which infests the snails eaten by the kites, is responsible for still further decline in the population.

Conservationists are trying to bring back this endangered species with educational programs and by expanding areas of freshwater marshes.

SHORT-WINGED BIRD HAWKS:
Subfamily *Accipitrinae*

While walking through the woods you may see one of the Short-winged Bird Hawks that live in wooded country over most of the United States. These forest hawks have relatively short, rounded wings and long tails, a form well adapted to flight among tree branches and through brush.

When hunting, they glide low, then flap their wings and dart rapidly about among the trees, chasing their prey. They also hunt by stealth, sitting perched until they sight their prey, then plunging down upon it.

While traveling, they may fly high with a steady, flapping wing beat, interspersed with sailings.

They have earned the name Bird Hawks because they, of all the hawks, prey mostly on birds, their principal food. They take song and game birds, and deserve the name Chicken and Pigeon Hawk. Although individuals of other hawk species do take poultry, it is the Short-winged Bird Hawks that most often raid hen yards and pigeon cotes. However, as we have already pointed out, since most commercial chicken growers now keep their poultry in hen houses and do not allow them to range, damage to chicken farmers from hawks is largely confined to family flocks.

The female Short-winged Bird Hawks are bigger than the males.

In the United States there are three species of the Bird Hawks or Accipiters, as they are often called.

GOSHAWK, CHICKEN HAWK, or HEN HAWK:
Accipiter gentilis

The name of this hawk is often mispronounced. It is Gos-hawk, not Gosh-hawk! The name is from an old English word meaning goose hawk.

The Goshawk is much the biggest of the three Accipiters, and a handsome bird. It has a wingspread of from forty-three to forty-seven inches. The male is twenty-two inches in length, and the female twenty-four inches.

The tail, like that of the Cooper's Hawk, is rounded.

To see a Goshawk strike is to see a wonder in speed. The bird may suddenly plunge from its perch in a tree, or while on the wing, may drop down on its prey. Because of its speed, falconers choose this hawk above all the other hawks that are not true falcons.

In the wild, the Goshawk preys on game birds, such as pheasants, and on small birds, and also takes wood-chucks, rabbits, mice, and insects.

The Goshawk has earned from farmers the name of Chicken and Hen Hawk, and when its home is near an open chicken yard, the bird lives up to its name.

The Goshawk usually nests in an evergreen tree, often at a great height, as much as seventy-five feet above the ground. It may build a new nest every year, or it may add to an old nest. The nesting material consists of twigs and sticks, lined with strips of bark and evergreen twigs. The female hawk usually lays three or four eggs.

Like the smaller Sharp-shinned Hawk, the Goshawk is in general slate-blue gray above and white below. The white is finely streaked and barred with slate color. The feathers on the head are black, but when the feathers on the back of the head are erected, white under feathers show.

There is a distinctive broad white stripe over each eye.

Although the young Goshawks have the character-istic white eyebrows of the adult, the younger birds are brown above and white below, with dark brown markings.

Goshawk

The Goshawk breeds from Alaska and northern Canada into the northern United States, and in the East as far south as Maryland. Unlike the other Short-winged Bird Hawks, it seems to be increasing in number.

Some Goshawks winter within their breeding range. Others fly south to the southern states, from Texas east to Virginia and sometimes Florida, and southward to Mexico.

SHARP-SHINNED HAWK: *Accipiter striatus*

The Sharp-shinned Hawk is the smallest of the three Short-winged Bird Hawks. It has a body about the size of a quail. The male is eleven inches in length, and the female twelve to fourteen inches. The wingspread is about twenty-one inches.

The Sharp-shinned Hawk is a fierce little bird. It preys on all sorts of small birds. It has been estimated by the U.S. Department of Agriculture, from an examination of the stomachs of dead hawks, that nearly 97 per cent of the Sharp-shinned's diet is made up of small birds. Although this hawk rarely attacks full-grown poultry, it will take young chickens which, we stress again, are allowed to range. It also preys on pigeons, and supplements its diet with a few mice and rabbits, frogs and insects.

Sharp-shinned Hawk

The Sharp-shinned Hawk usually nests in pine or other evergreen trees, about twenty to thirty feet above the ground. Most often it builds a new nest of sticks and twigs every year but sometimes uses an old nest again. There are usually four or five eggs.

31

The plumage of the adult bird is dark bluish-slate above and white below. The underparts and leg feathers are barred with reddish bands. The tail is barred with brownish-black bands and is square, not rounded, and slightly notched. The cere, the eyes, and the feet are yellow. The claws are black.

The young are dark brown above, and the underparts are dull yellowish to white, streaked and barred with brown.

The "Sharpies" breed from Alaska and Canada throughout the United States in wooded areas. They winter from southern Canada south to Panama.

COOPER'S HAWK: *Accipiter cooperii*

Cooper's Hawk is really a bigger edition of the Sharp-shinned. Except for its larger size and the cut of its tail, it looks like a Sharp-shinned. Its plumage is almost exactly the same. But its tail is rounded, not square, and the Cooper's Hawk has a wingspread of from thirty to thirty-six inches. The male measures eighteen inches in length, the female twenty inches.

Cooper's Hawk is rightly called a Chicken and Pigeon Hawk. Being larger than the Sharp-shinned, equally fast and fierce, and very wily, it is the terror of the open hen yard and dovecote. The birds do more damage than the Goshawk, not because they are better hunters but because they are more numerous.

Cooper's Hawk

It has been estimated by the Department of Agriculture that the diet of Cooper's Hawk is made up of 55 per cent small birds, 12 per cent game birds, 10 per cent poultry, 17 per cent rodents, 3.3 per cent insects, 1.7 per cent rabbits, and 1 per cent frogs.

Cooper's Hawks build nests of sticks and twigs ten to fifty feet above the ground in tall evergreen or deciduous trees. They often come back to the same nests for several years, adding new material each year until their nests are very bulky. Sometimes a Cooper's Hawk will nest in another hawk's old nest or in a crow's old nest. There are usually four or five eggs.

This hawk breeds from southern Canada south throughout the United States in wooded areas, and winters from southern Ontario through the United States and as far south as Mexico and Costa Rica.

BROAD-WINGED RODENT HAWKS or BUTEOS: Subfamily *Buteoninae*

From three to five of the outer primary feathers in the wings of the Broad-winged Rodent Hawks are deeply notched—wings suited to great, high, soaring flight. The tails are of medium length, and more or less fan-shaped when spread. Most of these hawks—Buteos as they are often called—are larger than the Accipiters.

Different species of the Broad-winged Rodent Hawks are found in wooded areas and mountains and on the open plains and deserts all over the United States.

There is a difference in size between the males and females as there is in the Short-winged Bird Hawks.

These are the most beneficial hawks to the farmers. A large part of their diet is made up of rodents—rats, various kinds of mice, and squirrels—rabbits, and other small animals injurious to crops. They also take some birds, amphibians, and insects, particularly grasshoppers.

There are thirteen species of Buteos in the United States.

RED-TAILED HAWK, BUZZARD HAWK, or HEN HAWK: *Buteo jamaicensis*

This big, handsome hawk is among the largest of the Buteos. It has a wingspread of from fifty to fifty-six inches and a medium long, wide red tail that is the clue to its identity. The male is twenty-two inches in length, the female twenty-four inches.

The Red-tailed Hawk is a very beneficial species, feeding mostly on injurious small mammals and insects. The United States Department of Agriculture, in a study made of hawk stomachs, has estimated that the western Red-tailed's diet is 55 per cent rodents, other than squirrels, 9.3 per cent squirrels and rabbits, 10.5 per cent insects, 9.2 per cent small birds, 6.1 per cent frogs and snakes, 2.1 per cent game birds, and 1.5 per cent water creatures. At the time the survey was made poultry accounted for 6.3 per cent of the diet, a figure which with today's sheltered chicken farms is probably lower.

The Red-tailed Hawk nests forty to seventy feet above the ground in tall trees. The large nest is made

Red-tailed Hawk

of twigs and sticks lined with grapevine bark, the inner strips of cedar bark, and sprigs of evergreen or moss. The female generally lays from two to three eggs.

The adult eastern Red-tailed is brown above, mixed with whitish and light brown on the crown, nape, and lower back. The plumage on the underparts is whitish and abdomen is streaked with dark brown. The wings have dark brown bars. The rufous, or reddish, tail is bordered near the terminal end with a narrow black band and is tipped with white. The bill is black, the cere, legs, and feet yellow, the eyes brown.

The young are heavily streaked with black on the abdomen. Their tails are gray with narrow black bars.

The Red-tailed Hawk of the Great Plains sometimes has a white tail. A darker phase occurs in other parts of the West.

The various phases of the Red-tailed Hawk are seen in wooded areas from Alaska and central and eastern Canada throughout the United States south to Mexico and Panama. The birds winter from southern Maine and the middle western states southward.

HARLAN'S HAWK: *Buteo harlani*

An uncommon hawk of the Northwest, Harlan's Hawk closely resembles the Red-tailed Hawk. Its length is twenty inches and the wingspread is around fifty inches.

There are two color phases. The adult plumage of the dark phase is mostly black, the tail mottled with rufous, white, and gray, and with a subterminal band of black. The light phase has white underparts, with brown on the belly and the sides of the breast.

Harlan's Hawk breeds from the Yukon and Alaska to northern British Columbia. It winters in the midwestern states south to Texas and Louisiana. It is occasional in California, Colorado, Illinois, Indiana, Mississippi, and Pennsylvania.

RED-SHOULDERED HAWK: *Buteo lineatus*

The Red-shouldered Hawk is a little smaller than the Red-tailed and not so heavy. The length of the male is twenty inches, that of the female twenty-two inches. The wingspread is from forty-four to fifty inches.

The Red-shouldered likes to lurk in the woods and is not so often seen as its Red-tailed counterpart, except in spring when it circles about, screaming lustily.

However, like the Red-tailed, it has been dubbed a Chicken and a Hen Hawk, these names doing the bird an injustice. It is one of the most valuable of our birds of prey. It has been estimated that about 90 per cent of its diet is made up of mammals, such as mice, and insects, both real enemies of the farmer. As for the rest of its diet, the bird is quite omnivorous, feeding on frogs, snakes, fish, spiders, snails, and earthworms, and now and then a game bird or a chicken.

Red-shouldered Hawk

The Red-shouldered Hawk usually nests in a tall deciduous tree. The nesting material is sticks. There are usually three to five eggs. The plumage of the adult bird is brown above with rufous streakings. The wings above are dark brown crossed with narrow whitish bands. The upper side of the tail is dark brown crossed by four or five whitish bars and is white tipped. The underparts are light rufous with buff white bars on the lower breast and belly. The throat is light tan streaked with brown. The bill is black, the cere and legs yellow, the eyes brown.

The young birds are darker on the back, with fewer streaks, and have white underparts streaked with brown.

The Red-shouldered Hawk is at home in woods and swampy tree areas over the eastern half of the United States. The Florida Red-shouldered Hawk is smaller than the common species and is seen in the South Atlantic and Gulf states. The Red-shouldered found in the valleys on the Pacific Coast is as big as the eastern hawk, but is more rufous on the underparts. The Red-shouldered winters over much of its range.

BROAD-WINGED HAWK: *Buteo platypterus*

This small, stout hawk has a wingspread of from thirty-three to thirty-eight inches. The males are fourteen inches in length, the females eighteen inches.

Broad-winged Hawk

The Broad-winged Hawk is a denizen of the deep woods. It likes solitude. It will sit perched on a limb of a tree, seemingly for hours, but when some prey moves below, it dives with lightning speed.

Like the other Buteos, it is a beneficial species. Its food consists mainly of mice and squirrels and other small mammals, frogs, insects, such as grasshoppers, crickets, beetles, and the caterpillars of big moths, and occasionally a bird.

The Broad-winged Hawk usually nests in trees from ten to eighteen feet above the ground. The nesting material is sticks and bark, lined with feathers and soft roots. The eggs number from two to five.

The color of the adult hawk is dark brown to gray-brown. The feathers on the back are edged with amber-brown. The tail has three grayish-white bars. The underparts are grayish, barred with reddish brown. The wings are white underneath. The cere and feet are yellow, the claws black, the beak very dark. The eyes are light reddish-hazel.

The young have streaks and dark spots on the under-parts, and their eyes are pale brown.

Broad-winged Hawks breed in Canada south to the Gulf coast of Florida. Some may winter in the Ohio and Delaware valleys and Florida, but most migrate in large flocks to South America.

SWAINSON'S HAWK: *Buteo swainsoni*

This hawk of western North America is a big hawk, though not quite as large as the Red-tailed. The male is about twenty inches in length, the female twenty-two inches. The spread of wings is up to fifty-six inches.

It is a very beneficial species.

A common hawk in the sagebrush country of the West and on the plains, it circles over this open country, looking for mice, gophers, and other small rodents, and insects, taking grasshoppers and black crickets, which are seasonally very harmful to farms in certain parts of the West. It rarely preys on birds.

Swainson's Hawk makes its nest of twigs, lined with softer materials, such as leaves or moss, in trees, bushes, or on the ground. There are usually two eggs.

There are two color phases. In the light phase, the adult is gray-brown above. The forehead and throat are white. The chest is cinnamon color and the rest of the underparts are white, faintly barred with brown. The tail has eight or nine narrow dark bands, and one broader terminal band. The bill and claws are black, the cere and feet yellow.

The rare melanistic phase has all dark brown plumage, except on the throat and the tail, which is banded. Every grade of color between the light and dark phases is seen in different individuals.

The upperparts of the young are brown except for the

Swainson's Hawk

head which is buff-colored. The underparts are also
buff, heavily marked with brown. The tail and wings
are barred.

Swainson's Hawk breeds from Alaska and northern
Canada south to Alberta and Saskatchewan and into
the United States as far east as Minnesota and south
into Texas and Baja California. In winter these hawks

migrate in great flocks through Mexico and as far south as Argentina.

Swainson's Hawk is occasionally seen in eastern North America.

ZONE-TAILED HAWK: *Buteo albonotatus*

This big but slender black Buteo of the Southwest is identified by its long black-and-white barred tail and by its flight, which resembles that of the Turkey Vulture. The male is nineteen inches in length, the female twenty-one inches. The wings are longer and more narrow than those of most Buteos. The wingspread is from forty-seven to fifty-three inches.

It nests in cottonwood, sycamore, and other trees that grow by stream beds in the wooded canyons it haunts. The nesting material is sticks lined with leaves or Spanish moss. The eggs number two to four.

The Zone-tailed Hawk often soars like a Turkey Vulture, tipping on wings held in a wide V. It preys on mice and rats and other small mammals, frogs and lizards and insects.

The adult plumage of this hawk is almost entirely glossy black, save for the tail bars mentioned above and the white markings on the underwings. The beak is dark dull yellow.

The young are very much like the adults, but show

white under feathers, particularly on the head and neck. Their tail bars are more numerous.

The Zone-tailed Hawk breeds in the Southwest in Arizona, New Mexico, and Texas, and, rarely, in southern California, south through Mexico and into northern South America. It winters through most of its breeding range.

Zone-tailed Hawk

WHITE-TAILED HAWK: *Buteo albicaudatus*

This large handsome hawk of Mexico and South America is rare north of the Mexican border, except in southern Texas. The length of the male is twenty-two inches, the female twenty-four inches. The wingspread is up to fifty-six inches.

The tail is conspicuously pure white, with a subterminal black band and fine black crosslines. The rump and wing coverts are also white. The plumage of the upperparts of the adult male is ash gray, with some red, particularly noticeable on the shoulders. The underparts are white, crossed with fine bars on the sides. The females are darker in plumage.

SHORT-TAILED HAWK: *Buteo brachyurus*

This hawk of Mexico and South America is resident locally in southern Florida. Its length is up to sixteen inches and the wingspread is about thirty-five inches. There are two color phases. The dark phase has dark brown to black plumage, a tail barred with olive gray, and sometimes a white mark on the forehead. The plumage of the upperparts of the light phase is dark brown with a white forehead. The tail is barred as in the dark phase. The underparts are white.

47

ROUGH-LEGGED HAWK: *Buteo lagopus*

The large Rough-legged Hawk is a nesting bird of the Arctic regions. The male is twenty inches in length, and the female twenty-two inches. The wingspread is about fifty-two inches. The feathers on the legs extend down to the feet.

It is the most nocturnal of our hawks, flying often at dusk.

The Rough-legged, one of the most beneficial of hawks, unfortunately visits the United States only in winter. According to a survey made by the U.S. Department of Agriculture, based on studies of hawk stomachs, the Rough-legged's diet consists of 72 per cent rodents other than squirrels, 8.6 per cent rabbits and squirrels, 6.5 per cent insects, 4.3 per cent small birds, 4.3 per cent game birds, 2.2 per cent water creatures, and 2.1 per cent snakes and frogs.

This hawk is at home in open and brushy country. In the treeless country where it breeds, it will make its nest of twigs and weeds and grasses on cliffs. The female usually lays two or three eggs, and both the male and female take turns incubating.

The color of the plumage of an adult Rough-legged Hawk varies greatly. There are light and melanistic phases, and other phases in between. The adult of the light phase has grayish-brown plumage above with buff

Rough-legged Hawk

or whitish underparts streaked and barred with dark brown. The white tail has a broad dark band. The eyes are brown, the beak black, and the feet yellow. The melanistic phase has dark brown underparts with white on sections of the underwings, and a white tail with a dark band.

The young are quite like the adults but are not so heavily marked.

The Rough-legged Hawk breeds in the Far North, in Alaska and Labrador and Canada. It is seen in the United States only in the wintertime, when it may migrate as far south as California and Arizona and Oklahoma in the West and rarely as far as Tennessee in the East.

FERRUGINOUS HAWK: Buteo regalis

The uncommon Ferruginous Hawk is very similar to the Rough-legged. It, too, has a light and a dark phase, but the white tail of the Ferruginous lacks the dark band of the Rough-legged. The light phase is light brown above with streaks of white and brown. The underparts are white, and the feathers on the legs rufous.

Like the Rough-legged, it is a beneficial species. According to the Department of Agriculture survey, the prey of the Ferruginous is 54 per cent rodents other than squirrels, 29 per cent rabbits and squirrels, 9 per cent insects, 4 per cent small birds, and 4 per cent game birds.

The Ferruginous Hawk, largest of the Buteos, breeds from south central Canada south into Washington, Oregon, New Mexico, Texas, and Oklahoma. They sometimes winter as far north as their most northern range, but more often migrate to the Southwest of the United States and southward into Mexico.

GRAY HAWK: *Buteo nitidus*

This small gray hawk of South America and Mexico is also resident in our Southwest, in southern Arizona, southern New Mexico, and southern Texas. The adult plumage is in general gray, but with light streaks and bars on the upperparts. The tail is brown, white tipped, and crossed with one or two white bands. The underparts are white barred with gray. The length is up to fifteen inches with a wingspread of about thirty-five inches.

HARRIS' HAWK: *Parabuteo unicinctus*

Harris' Hawk is a big southwestern hawk with large feet and long black, curved claws. Its very dark plumage appears entirely black when the bird is in flight, except for the conspicuous white rump, white undertail coverts, and broad white terminal band on the tail, good identification points. The male is twenty inches in length, the female twenty-three inches. The wingspread is forty-three inches. The bird is Buteo-like with long, broad wings, and Buteo-like, it sometimes soars. But other times it hunts more like a Goshawk, low over the ground. Its favorite habitat is arid and semiarid sagebrush country. Its favorite foods are wood rats, chipmunks, rabbits, and other small mammals, and small snakes and lizards. It also preys on birds and rarely eats carrion.

Harris' Hawk makes its nest of sticks and leaves lined with grass, or Spanish moss where available, and other soft material. Its nesting site is often a yucca plant, a mesquite tree, or one of the giant cactus plants common to its range. There are usually three or four eggs. Both sexes take turns incubating the eggs as well as feeding the young.

Viewed close up, the plumage of the adult is very dark brown with darker tail and wings. In addition to the white markings mentioned above, there is considerable rufous color on the shoulders and beautiful bright rufous feathers on the thighs. The lores—the spaces

Harris' Hawk

between the eyes and the beak—are nearly naked, save for a few sparse bristles. The beak is blue-gray, the cere and lores yellow, the eyes reddish brown, the legs and feet orange. The young are more brownish and streaked with a yellowish color on the head and neck. The underparts are white streaked with brown, the thigh feathers white and barred.

This is a hawk of our Southwest, also seen occasionally in Iowa, Ohio, Louisiana, and Mississippi. Some live all year around in their breeding range, though often they migrate in winter south of the Mexican border.

BLACK HAWK: *Buteogallus anthracinus*

Still another hawk commonly resident south of the Mexican border is the Black Hawk. It is a hawk of Mexico and northern South America, occasionally resident in our Southwest—in southern New Mexico, Arizona, and in the Rio Grande Valley in Texas.

The Black Hawk's wings and tail are even broader than the average Buteo's. The length is up to twenty inches, the wingspread forty-eight inches. The adult plumage is mostly black with some brown markings.

In flight the adult may be identified by its tail, which is black with one or two white bands, and by the white marks on the undersurface of the wings.

EAGLES: Subfamily *Buteoninae*

Eagles are related to the Buteo Hawks, belonging to the same subfamily. They are, of course, much larger than the hawks. They have the same broad wings, and they soar as do the Buteos.

GOLDEN EAGLE: *Aquila chrysaetos*

The very large, powerful Golden Eagle has the broad, rounded wings of the Buteos, and the same grand soaring flight. It has a wingspread of up to seven and a half feet and is about three feet in length.

When falconry was popular in the Old World, the Golden Eagle was reserved for use by kings, mostly for hunting foxes or other mammals rather than birds, because an eagle is not as agile as the smaller falcons.

In the wilds of its homeland the Golden Eagle feeds on squirrels, prairie dogs, gophers, and other small rodents, hares and rabbits, foxes, game and other birds, and snakes. It may also prey on larger animals, such as the lambs of mountain sheep, the kids of mountain goats, and the fawns of deer. When living near ranches or farms, it will also attack the young of domestic stock, such as lambs, calves, and pigs.

The Golden Eagle makes its nest of big sticks lined with grasses and weeds on a high cliff or sometimes in a

55

tall tree. It may return to the same nest every year, adding material until sometimes the nest is five feet across and almost as high. There are two eggs. The female does most of the incubation but the male sometimes takes a turn.

The adult plumage is dark brown with golden neck feathers. There is some white on the tail and some mottled white on the wings. The yellow toes are very large and strong. The powerful legs and the cere are yellow. The eyes are brown, the beak black.

At this, the adult age, it is easy to distinguish a Golden Eagle from an adult Bald Eagle, which has a striking white head, neck, and tail feathers.

When viewed from a distance, the young of the Golden Eagle, however, can easily be confused with the young of the Bald Eagle. Both are more or less dark brown or black. The juvenile (first year) Golden Eagle is mostly black, though its tail is banded with white and bordered with black. The immature (two to three years old) Golden Eagle has white patches under the wings. The tail is mostly white with a dark terminal band.

When viewed close up, it is easy to identify the young of both species. For the Golden Eagle's lower legs are feathered right down to the toes, while half of the lower legs of the Bald Eagle are bare.

Golden Eagle

The Golden Eagle is an uncommon bird of remote mountain areas and open country and deserts from northern Alaska south through Canada and into the United States to South Dakota and Texas, and on the west coast to Baja California and Mexico. Much less common in the East, it is occasionally seen in New York and the New England States.

The Golden Eagle usually lives all year within its breeding range. The northern birds migrate only when periodic food shortages cause them to move southward during the winter, at which time they may be seen as far south as Louisiana and northern Florida.

BALD EAGLE or AMERICAN EAGLE: *Haliaeetus leucocephalus*

This majestic bird is handsome when perching and magnificent in soaring flight. It often soars in circles on flatly extended wings to immense heights. Then it may go into a steep dive, with half-closed wings. It has a wingspread of up to seven feet. The length of the male is thirty to thirty-five inches, the female thirty-four to forty-three.

This bird is called the Bald Eagle because of its snow-white head. It was named the American Eagle when, in 1782, the Continental Congress of the United States adopted it as our national emblem. As such, this eagle now appears on the Great Seal of the United

States, the presidential seal, and others, and on many U.S. coins.

The Bald Eagle is a fish eagle, subsisting mainly on fish. It has very keen eyesight. When fishing, it often sits patiently on a tree limb until it spots its prey near the surface of the water. Or it may hover on slow-beating wings over shallow water until it sees a school of fish. Then it dives but, unlike the Osprey, it usually does not submerge; it gets the fish by dipping only its feet in the water. Its staple is dead or dying fish.

The Bald Eagle delights in stealing fish from its cousin, the Osprey, which is a much better fisherman anyway. After the Osprey has risen with a fish in its claws, the eagle devils the bird by chasing it, forcing it ever higher and higher in the air until the Osprey, in desperation, drops its prey which the eagle promptly catches. The eagle is clever, too, in locating schools of fish by following gulls and other fish-eating birds.

The Bald Eagle takes dead fish found on the shore or floating in water any chance it gets. In Alaska great numbers of these eagles gather along the shores of rivers when the salmon and herring are running upstream to spawn. Then they, along with the big brown bears, feast on the dead fish cast on shore after spawning.

The Bald Eagle is seen along the shores of rivers and lakes where it finds its favorite food. When fish are scarce, it will take other food—birds and small to quite

Bald Eagle

large animals, crabs, turtles, and snakes, even carrion.

The Bald Eagle nests in tall pines or tall deciduous trees, such as elms and hickories, and sometimes in Florida in cypress trees. The nest is built twenty to one hundred and twenty feet above the ground. In Alaska, where tall trees are scarce, it often nests on cliffs or rocks.

The nest is made of large sticks and lined with weeds and other soft material, such as cornstalks and, in the South, Spanish moss. Each year a pair of eagles will return to their old nest and add more material so that an old Bald Eagle nest may be very large and bulky indeed.

The neck, the head, and the tail of an adult Bald Eagle are snowy white in color. The rest of the plumage is dark brown, with feather edgings of olive gray. The powerful beak is yellow, as are the cere, feet, and eyes.

During the first year of the Bald Eagle's life (juvenile) its plumage, head included, is black except for the underwing coverts and undertail, which are mottled white. The bill is black, the eyes brown. In the second and third year (immature) the plumage is mostly brown, the head and neck black. The bill is dark dull yellow, the eyes brown. The young look very much like the young of the Golden Eagle, but, as we have seen, they may be distinguished by their legs. Half of the Bald

Eagle's lower legs are bare, while the legs of the Golden Eagle are feathered to the toes.

The Bald Eagle is now endangered with extinction in the south. It was formerly found in the southern states west to California and into Mexico. Its present nesting area is mainly by estuaries of the Atlantic and Gulf coasts, from New Jersey west to Texas, south to Florida, and in the lower Mississippi Valley south from Arkansas and Tennessee.

The causes of the decline in numbers of these eagles are multiple: the increase in the development of housing in nesting areas and the disturbance of nesting birds; illegal shooting; and, very probably most important, the reduction of fertility caused by the pesticides taken in the food of adult birds.

The southern Bald Eagles are protected by law in sanctuaries now being established. Eight of the National Wildlife Refuges in the Southeast have Bald Eagles nesting there, and the Florida Audubon Society has enlisted support of landowners of 2,300,000 acres of private land where eagles nest. This area is now an eagle sanctuary.

The northern Bald Eagles are migratory only when the waters where they obtain their food freeze over. The young of the southern Bald Eagles may go north for a time, after they have left the nest.

HARRIERS: Subfamily *Circinae*

MARSH HAWK: *Circus cyaneus*

What we commonly call in America today a Marsh Hawk might more correctly be called a Marsh Harrier, for that is what it is, the one and only member of the harrier group in our country. Like other harriers, the Marsh Hawk is characterized by its habit of flying low over marsh and open grasslands with tilting wings held above the horizontal, hunting, back and forth, much in the manner of a harrier dog, a hare hound.

Marsh Hawk

The Marsh Hawk is a fairly large bird, with a length of up to twenty-two inches and a wingspread of up to fifty-two inches. The head has a distinct owl-like facial disc and ruff.

According to a survey made by the U. S. Department of Agriculture, based on studies of hawk stomachs, including those of the Marsh Hawk, this harrier makes up 41 per cent of its diet on small birds, 33 per cent on rodents other than squirrels, 9 per cent squirrels and rabbits, 7.2 per cent game birds, 4.1 per cent frogs, 3.3 per cent insects, 2.3 per cent poultry, and 1 per cent aquatic creatures.

The Marsh Hawk makes its nest of marsh grasses on the ground. The number of eggs is usually two to six.

The wings of the Marsh Hawk are long and narrow, but not as pointed as a falcon's. The tail is long, and so are the legs, which are bare below.

There is a marked difference in the color of the plumage between the sexes. The white rump is conspicuous in both the female and the male, and is an important point of identification when this harrier is observed in flight. Otherwise the female is brown with yellowish or white markings. Her tail is broadly banded in brown. The underparts are white streaked with brown. The male is similar in markings to the female but his plumage is gray and white.

The beak is black, the cere and legs yellow. The eyes

64

of the female are brownish, those of the male yellow.

The young are similar to the adult female but cinnamon in color below.

The Marsh Hawk is a common hawk in marsh and other open grasslands over a large territory. It breeds from Alaska through Canada, Labrador, and Newfoundland, south to our southwestern states and Kansas and Virginia. It winters from southern Canada south in the United States to northern South America.

OSPREY:
Family *Pandionidae*

OSPREY or FISH HAWK: Pandion haliaetus

This large, eagle-like bird has a wingspread of up to five and a half feet. The wings are long and pointed, good wings for hovering over water—and this is a water-loving species. The length is from twenty-two to twenty-four inches.

Of interest to the bird watcher with binoculars, the Osprey has a special manner of soaring that distinguishes it, even at a great distance, from the Bald Eagle, which soars flat winged, and the Turkey Vulture, which soars with upwardly inclined wings. When outspread the Osprey's wings have a crook in the middle.

As its second common name indicates, it is a Fish Hawk. Fish is its main food.

Osprey

The Osprey finds its food mostly in shallow waters. While fishing, it hovers with wings flapping, then dives toward the water head first. At the last second it throws its feet forward to catch its prey on or near the surface of the water. The bird plummets down so fast and raises such a spray on contact with the water that it is difficult to see what happens. The Osprey may submerge for an instant but does not dive deep. It rises from the water with the fish clasped in its feet, which are well adapted for fishing.

They are large, with sharp little projections on the soles, and the claws are very long and curved. Furthermore the Osprey can move the outer toe forward or backward at will, as can the owls. The feet are admirably formed for catching fish.

The home of the Osprey is near the seacoast or by some large body of water.

The Osprey might be dubbed the most higgledy-piggledy nest builder. It starts its large, bulky, clumsy-looking nest usually with long sticks, often driftwood, and may incorporate anything at hand, including bones, old clothing, and old shoes. It lines the nest with softer material such as seaweed and moss. It lays two to four eggs.

The site it selects for nesting depends upon the region in which it lives. The nest is often high up and sometimes bizarre. When the bird lives in canyon country, such as Yellowstone National Park, it may build on a rocky pinnacle. It commonly builds in tall trees, often choosing a dead one, but at times it nests very low down, on a hunter's blind for example or even on the ground, perhaps in an old discarded box.

In Rhode Island and on Long Island when tall dead trees became scarce the Ospreys started building their nests on the double-cross arms at the top of power line poles. While dragging wet seaweed across the power lines, the birds short-circuited the wires with disastrous results for the Ospreys and the lines.

To remedy this nuisance, the power companies set up separate poles with platforms and added presents of sticks; or they made extensive platforms from the existing power poles. The Ospreys at once took these man-made nesting sites.

The adult plumage of an Osprey is dark brown above. The head and nape are white streaked with black and with broad dark markings on the sides of the head. The head feathers can be raised. The underparts are white, save for the breast which has brown heart-shaped marks. These marks are more numerous on the female than on the male. The tail is barred. The beak is black, the cere and legs bluish gray, the eyes yellow.

In the young, the head is darker and there are white edgings on the feathers of the upper parts.

68

Unlike most birds of prey, Ospreys may live in quite large colonies. They breed from Alaska throughout Canada and the United States wherever they find water suitable to their needs. They were once common on the Atlantic Coast and on the Florida Gulf coast but their numbers in these areas are declining, probably as a result of pesticides that are present in fish that they take in contaminated waters. For example, in 1954 there were 164 nests counted along the Connecticut River. In 1967 the count was down to 11 nests.

Ospreys are migratory and winter in our southern states and southward into South America.

CARACARAS and FALCONS:
Family *Falconidae*

CRESTED or COMMON CARACARA, AUDUBON'S CARACARA: Caracara cheriway

This long-legged, long-tailed scavenger, the only Caracara in our country, is very closely related to—in fact belongs to the same family as—the falcons. It has long, narrow blunt wings. However, though its head is not lacking in feathers, its face resembles that of a vulture. The skin is bare and red. The length of the Crested

Caracara is up to twenty-five inches and the wingspread up to forty-eight inches.

The habits of the Caracara are more like those of a vulture than a falcon. It hunts in prairie and open brush land, looking for carrion, its main food. When hunting for dead animals, it may circle high, then flap its wings. Incidentally, the Caracaras often associate with vultures. They also may roost in trees, with three or four other Caracaras, but they spend much of their time on the ground, either sitting or running about looking for live prey. They take living mice, lizards, insects, and grubs, as well as carrion.

They also get food by attacking other birds, particularly pelicans, and taking their prey away from them. The Caracara will go after a pelican and force it to disgorge its pouchful of fish.

Caracaras build large nests of sticks and grasses in trees and bushes—in Florida often in the Cabbage Palmetto. There are two or three eggs.

Their hoarse, rattling cry sounds somewhat like their name.

The upper parts of the adult, including the crest, are black. The neck color is white or buff. The tail is white with narrow brown bars and a broad brown band at the tip. The breast is white with brown spots. The lower underparts are black. The cere, like the bare face, is red. The bill is long and hooked and bluish white in color.

Crested Caracara

The bare lower legs are yellow, the toes and talons very long. The eyes are red-brown.

The plumage of the young is browner with darker markings and up and down streaks, rather than bars.

All of the Caracaras are tropical birds. The only one coming into the southern United States is this species, the Crested Caracara, which is seen in Arizona, New Mexico, Texas, and southern Florida.

FALCONRY

Falconry is the very ancient sport of hunting game with hawks. Falconry is also, and rightly, called hawking.

The most popular and most commonly used birds for this sport are true falcons (*Falco*). Certain hawks that are not true falcons but true hawks (*Accipiter*) are also popular. A few of the Broad-winged Hawks (*Buteo*) are sometimes used, and also eagles.

So falconry and hawking mean the same thing.

In speaking of a falcon, a falconer generally says "she." This is because the females are most often chosen because of their larger size. To the initiated, the males are known as tiercels—they are a third smaller than the females.

Falconry probably started in Asia as long ago as 2000 B.C. or even earlier and was very probably first practiced, not as a sport, but as a means of obtaining food and perhaps also as a means of killing off predators. In Mongolia the Golden Eagle is still used to kill wolves.

The sport of falconry was taken up in Europe around A.D. 400 to 500 and became a serious sport in England after the Norman Conquest in 1066, at which time the rank of an Englishman could be told by the falcon he carried on his fist. The Gyrfalcon and the Peregrine

Falcon were traditionally reserved for nobility. The eagle, though not so fast, was reserved for kings. The priest carried an Old World Kestrel (Sparrow Hawk), while a commoner would often be seen, not with a true falcon but with an Old World Goshawk (genus *Accipiter*).

Falconry is practiced today with most of the trappings used by falconers in Shakespeare's day, which in turn were introduced to the Continent and England from the Orient. There is the glove for the fist on which the falcon sits; the leash, or creance, as the falconer says; the bells attached to the falcon's legs; and the hood that is slipped over the bird's head to keep it quiet while being taken into the field. These hoods are quaint and decorative, and in the days when royalty practiced the sport were often jeweled.

The training of a hawk, or manning as the experts say, is carried out by kindness and rewards of food. A falcon is always kept hungry just before training time, and is taken hungry into the field. The bird is rewarded by the falconer after the kill.

Falcons are called hawks of the lure because they are trained by the use of a leather pad with two thongs to which are attached pieces of meat or merely tufts of fur or feathers. The falconer teaches the bird first to come to the lure from nearby, then from a distance.

The hawks that are not true falcons are called hawks of the fist. They do not ascend to great heights as do the falcons, and they are taught to return directly to the fist for a reward of meat.

A falconer takes his hooded bird and a bird dog into the field. The dog points a pheasant, the falcon is released and mounts high in the sky. Then the dog flushes the pheasant and the falcon descends with a breathtaking dive to strike the quarry. The bells help tell the falconer where the falcon is with its prey.

In the United States falconry was started at the beginning of this century. In 1964 the Secretary of the Interior amended the Migratory Bird Treaty Act Regulations, making it legal to use falcons to hunt all species of migratory game birds, except where prohibited by state law. The North American Falconers Association promotes the sport in North America.

FALCONS: Subfamily *Falconinae*

Falcons are among the most fierce, as well as among the most famous, birds of prey. And they are the swiftest. They fly with a rapid wing beat.

Falcons have neat, streamlined bodies, long, pointed wings, and quite long tails, a form well suited for hunting in the open country, where they live. The heads are small with moustache-like stripes on the sides. The toes are long.

The female falcons are larger than the males.

The beak of a falcon is especially to be noted for it is distinctly notched. A falcon stuns a flying bird by diving down on or up under it, and striking forcefully with open feet. When the falcon has its prey on the ground, if the prey is not already dead, the falcon kills it by breaking the neck with its beak. Falcons, and hawks too, often mantle—that is hover over a fallen prey—making sure that no other bird or animal is going to try to take their catch away.

GYRFALCON: *Falco rusticolus*

This large Arctic bird is the pride of the falconer, though it is not used for falconry as often as the Peregrine because it is more difficult to obtain and to keep healthy.

The Gyrfalcon looks very tall when perched, its tallness being emphasized by the rather long tail. The length of the female is twenty-four inches, the male twenty-one inches. The wingspread is fifty inches and sometimes more. Like most birds of prey of the Far North, the legs are heavily feathered down to the toes.

The Gyrfalcon hunts flying low over the Arctic tundra, over the open plains and mountain plateaus. It preys on ptarmigan, auks, puffins, ducks, gulls, grouse, and other northern birds, and will also take lemmings and ground squirrels.

Gyrfalcon

These falcons, like others, make no nests. They lay their eggs in little depressions on cliffs or sometimes use old raven or hawk nests. The female lays from two to four eggs.

There are three distinct color phases: the common gray phase, the white phase occurring mostly in Greenland, and the dark phase of western Canada. The gray phase (adult) is grayish-brown above. The feathers are edged with white and the tail and wings are barred. The white underparts are streaked with dark gray-brown.

The dark phase is similar in markings but with some black on the underwings.

The white phase has white plumage all over, marked with brown.

The cere and legs are yellow, the beak bluish, the eyes brown.

The young of the common gray phase have more white on the head and the edges of the feathers than the adults. The young of the dark phase have dark underparts with white streaks. The young of the white phase have darker markings.

The Gyrfalcon is strictly a polar species. In North America its range includes Alaska, Greenland, and Canada. It often winters within its range. Rarely it may migrate into the United States along the Canadian border.

PRAIRIE FALCON: *Falco mexicanus*

The brown Prairie Falcon is not as big as the Gyrfalcon but it is very fast. The male measures eighteen inches in length, the female twenty inches. The wingspread is up to forty inches.

It is at home in prairie lands and deserts, where it hunts birds and small mammals.

Prairie Falcon

It nests usually on a cliff, but sometimes on a high riverbank. The eggs number from three to five.

The adult Prairie Falcon is brown above, the forehead and throat white. The bird is white below with brown markings. The beak and cere are yellow, the claws black, and the eyes brown.

The young are darker above and more spotted below than the adults.

The Prairie Falcon breeds on the prairies of southern British Columbia, Alberta, and Saskatchewan in Canada, south to North Dakota and into the Southwest. It is sometimes seen in the midwestern states.

It winters within its breeding range and south into Mexico.

PEREGRINE FALCON or DUCK HAWK: *Falco peregrinus*

The Peregrine Falcon is a favorite of and the commonest of the falcons used by the falconers. It is a smaller bird than the Gyrfalcon, but almost as fast. The length of the male is eighteen inches, the female nineteen inches. The wingspread is forty inches.

The Peregrine feeds almost entirely on birds—songbirds, pigeons, grouse, pheasants, and ducks and other water fowl.

It is exciting to watch the aerial display of a Peregrine hunting. The Peregrine often circles so high in the air that it can scarcely be seen from the ground. It has such keen eyesight that it can spot a bird flying a thousand or more feet below.

When the Peregrine sights a bird, it dives down at terrific speed or, as the falconer says, it "stoops" and hits its prey, falcon fashion, sometimes from beneath, with its feet, and with such force that a bigger bird than itself—a pheasant for example—is immediately stunned. Then on the ground, if necessary, it kills, falcon fashion, by breaking the bird's neck with its beak.

Peregrines nest on cliffs or sometimes in holes in trees with no nesting materials. There are three or four eggs.

The upperparts of the adult are slate-blue in color, barred with brown. The beak is blue, the cere and legs yellow, the eyes brown. The female is much more heavily barred than the male.

The young have brown upperparts and yellowish underparts heavily marked with brown.

The range of the Peregrine Falcons is almost worldwide. In the Western Hemisphere the range is from Alaska to Greenland, south to Tierra del Fuego at the tip end of South America, but the falcons are absent as nesters from Mexico to Argentina. They winter from the northern states southward. In recent years, however, the Peregrines have become practically extinct in the

Peregrine Falcon

eastern United States and quite rare in some other parts of their range. Now the birds are most numerous in Alaska and northern Canada.

The decline in numbers is believed to be largely due to man's extensive use of pesticides. The Peregrines ingest these poisons in the prey they kill, and the pesticides either kill the falcons directly or cause the eggs to be infertile.

Peregrines are now protected by law in most of the states.

APLOMADO FALCON: *Falco femoralis*

The Aplomado Falcon is rare in the United States, coming over the Mexican border only occasionally into Arizona, New Mexico, and southern Texas.

The upperparts are gray. This falcon has black wings and a long black tail, both barred with white. The breast and flanks are white or yellowish with black markings. The rest of the underparts are orange. There is a white stripe over each eye. The bird's length is about fifteen inches, the wingspread thirty-five inches.

PIGEON HAWK or MERLIN: *Falco columbarius*

This uncommon little falcon looks like a small Peregrine Falcon and is like the Peregrine in its habits. It is trimly built with characteristically pointed falcon wings

Pigeon Hawk

that distinguish it from the also small Sharp-shinned Hawk that has short, rounded wings.

The length of the male is eleven inches, the female thirteen inches. The wingspread is twenty-three inches.

The Pigeon Hawk feeds mostly on birds. It hunts in open areas.

The female lays her four to five eggs in natural tree cavities, in holes in dirt banks, or in old nests of other birds. The birds use no nesting materials.

In this species the sexes are marked differently. The

83

upperparts of the male are mostly slate-colored, the head collared with white and spotted with brown. The eyebrows and cheeks are white with black streaks. The underparts are whitish with streaks of black or brown. The tail is barred with brown.

The female is dusky grayish-brown above with white collar and white and yellow bars on the tail. The underparts are like those of the male. In both sexes the bill is blue-gray, the cere yellow, the eyes brown.

The young are marked like the adult female but are plain brown above.

The Pigeon Hawk breeds across the northern states and Canada and up through Alaska. It winters sometimes in southern Canada into the northern states but more often migrates into the southern states and southward to the West Indies.

SPARROW HAWK or KESTREL: *Falco sparverius*

This is the smallest falcon. It has a body about the size of a quail. The female measures about eleven inches in length; the male is a little smaller. The wing-spread is up to twenty-one inches.

The Sparrow Hawk has the typical narrow, pointed Falcon wings. The bird may be identified by the rufous color of its back and tail, for it is the only *small* falcon with this plumage.

Characteristic is its habit of hovering with fast beating wings in one place. When perching it often jerks its tail.

It is a common hawk in open country and is a very beneficial species, feeding heavily on grasshoppers and other insects and caterpillars and switching to mice and sparrows in winter. According to a survey made by the U. S. Department of Agriculture, based on studies of hawk stomachs, the Sparrow Hawk's diet is made up of 63.5 per cent insects, 20.3 per cent rodents, 8.4 per cent small birds, 7.8 per cent frogs and snakes.

The Sparrow Hawk nests in cavities in trees, old woodpecker holes, cavities in rocks, and niches in old buildings, without nesting material. There are four or five eggs.

Both the adult male and the female have the same striking black and white markings on the face and a rufous patch on the top of the head. The upperparts of both sexes are rufous, barred with black. Only the male has slate-blue markings on the wings. Both male and female have white-tipped rufous tails, but the tail of the male has one broad black band, that of the female several narrow black bands. The underparts are whitish with dark brown spots and streaks. The breast feathers are suffused with very pale brown. The legs and cere are yellow, the bill blue-black, and the eyes dark brown.

The young are similar to the adult.

Sparrow Hawk

The range of the Sparrow Hawk is from Alaska and Canada south throughout the United States and into South America. The birds winter from southern British Columbia south to the Gulf Coast of the United States and on into Mexico and South America.

NOCTURNAL BIRDS
OF PREY:
Owls

ORDER *STRIGIFORMES*

Owls are really quite different, both in form and habits, from the members of the Order *Falconiformes*. Owls have big heads, and their facial characteristics set them apart from the diurnal birds of prey. The area around the eyes, the facial disc, is bordered with a ruff of feathers. The large, penetrating eyes look directly forward and are fixed in their sockets—an owl must turn its head to see to its right or left.

The thick neck plumage and short neck makes an owl appear to have no neck at all.

The feet differ, too, from those of the diurnal birds of prey. While the hawks have three toes that point permanently forward, and one hindward, in the owls, the fourth, the outer toe, may be moved forward or backward at will.

87

Some owls have ear tufts or "horns." Others are round-headed, with no ear tufts. The tails of most owls are relatively short.

You might well say that owls, like the members of the Order *Falconiformes,* come in many different sizes. There is the Great Gray Owl that is almost two feet in length and has a wingspread of five feet, and there is the tiny Elf Owl that is only five and a quarter inches in length and has a fifteen-inch wingspread. There are many different sizes in between.

Those of you who are bird watchers may not be able to observe owls as often as you would like, because most owls sleep during the daylight hours and fly at night. Only a few are active during the day. It is believed that owls can see well in the dark, although some owls are said to be guided, not entirely by sight, but also by extremely keen hearing.

The flight of owls is usually wavering, but sometimes they sail, and a few may hover like a hawk. Nearly all fly as silently as do bats. They fluff out their soft, thick feathers and wing their way noiselessly over the Arctic tundra, through the forests, over the plains and deserts, and over the high mountains, where different species live.

But even if you do not see too many owls, you cannot help but hear them. Their voices are far from noiseless. Many have very loud booming calls, and others screech.

Like hawks, owls are beneficial to man. Among their favorite prey are mice and rats, which, like the owls, are night creatures.

Owls are early nesters. Different species nest in a variety of locations, from tall trees to cliffs. Some species prefer barns and other outbuildings for their nesting sites. Others use cavities in trees. Still others like to take over abandoned hawk, crow, or squirrel nests. A few nest directly on the ground, while one species makes its nursery in a hole in the ground. Few actually build a nest.

There are two families of Nocturnal Birds of Prey: the Barn Owls (Family *Tytonidae*), with only one species in this country; and the Typical Owls (Family *Strigidae*), to which belong all of the other species living south of Canada and north of Mexico.

BARN OWL:
Family *Tytonidae*

BARN OWL or MONKEY-FACED OWL: Tyto alba

This big, distinctive, and odd-looking owl, with the heart-shaped facial disc and very long legs, has extremely keen hearing that enables it to catch prey on the darkest of nights. Scientists believe that the deeply dished facial disc helps to focus faint sounds.

The length of the Barn Owl is eighteen inches, the

Barn Owl

wingspread forty-four inches. There are no ear tufts.

This is the only member of Family *Tytonidae* in our area.

It is a beneficial species, a great mouser. It feeds mainly on mice of all kinds. It also takes gophers and shrews and sometimes catches a mole or a small bird.

As its name implies, the Barn Owl likes to nest in barns, also in other outbuildings, in towers, in cavities in trees, or in holes in a bank. The eggs usually number five to seven.

There are light and dark color phases. In the adult the plumage in the light phase is unusually bright for an owl. The upperparts are orange-buff and gray-brown mottled with white, and on the tail and wings barred with brown. The underparts are white, sparsely dotted with brown. The conspicuous eye discs are also white, faintly tinged with purple. The lower legs are sparsely feathered with very short feathers.

Another phase is lighter still, with completely white underparts. A darker phase has light orange underparts.

The long, curved beak is yellow, the eyes are black. This and the Barred Owl are the only owls that do not have yellow eyes.

The plumage of the young is very like that of the adult bird.

The Barn Owl, though not common, is at home over a wide range of territory. It may be seen from southern Canada south through the United States and on into Mexico and to the tip end of South America.

TYPICAL OWLS:
Family *Strigidae*

SCREECH OWL: Otus asio

The wailing, quivering cry of this small owl is known to most people in the United States, for it is a common owl in our country. The Screech Owl has a wingspread of twenty-two inches, and a length of from eight to ten inches. The bird is easy to identify, for it is the only small owl with tufted ears.

The Screech Owl is a beneficial species. Nearly three quarters of its food consists of insects and injurious small mammals. It feeds on grasshoppers, beetles and other insects, mice and squirrels, frogs and toads, and crawfish, and takes only a small percentage of birds.

It nests in cavities in trees, in abandoned woodpecker holes, and in barns, woodsheds, and other outbuildings. It is a common owl on farms and in orchards.

There are two color phases, the gray and the red. In the gray phase the adult is gray above, streaked and mottled with dark brown and white. The facial disc is white with narrow brown bars. The ruff is brown. The underparts are white, streaked and barred with brown.

The red phase is much like the gray in markings,

Screech Owls

except that rufous color everywhere replaces the gray and brown. In the red phase the bird is unmistakable, for it is the only owl with rufous plumage.

The beak is blue with a yellow tip; the eyes and toes are yellow.

Both the gray and the red phase occur in the East and also in southern Texas. In other parts of the West, there is a gray phase and a brown, rather than a red phase. The Screech Owls of the desert are generally paler in color.

A gray adult may mate with another gray adult or with a red. Two gray (or red) parents may have gray and red young; or the gray or red pair may have young of one color only.

The young are light in color and barred, not streaked.

The Screech Owl is at home from southeastern Alaska and southern Canada across the United States and south to Florida and Baja California.

The Whiskered Owl, or Spotted Screech Owl (*Otus trichopsis*), looks very much like and is closely related to the Screech Owl, but it is smaller. There is a gray and red phase but the plumage is darker. The Whiskered Owl is resident in the mountains from Arizona south into Mexico.

The Flammulated Owl (*Otis flammeolus*), another close relative of the Screech Owl, has very short ear tufts. There is a gray and a red phase, both being mottled with black.

GREAT HORNED OWL, BIG HOOT OWL or TIGER OF THE AIR: *Bubo virginianus*

This very large, robust owl is the only large owl with conspicuous "horns"—ear tufts—on its head. It measures twenty inches or more in length and has a wing-spread of sixty inches. Its feet are huge with great, curved, vicious black claws. The partial facial disc gives

94

Great Horned Owl

it a fierce look. When this owl calls in the night, *"whoo, whoo, whoo,"* with three, five, or six even notes, the woods fairly tremble, for the Great Horned Owl has a loud, deep voice, and it is as powerful, bloodthirsty, and savage as it looks and sounds.

Well named the Tiger of the Air, its call strikes terror into the hearts of wildlife. But when it is ready to strike, it swoops down on noiseless wings to seize its prey—mice, rats, squirrels, woodchucks, prairie dogs, muskrats, song and game birds, insects, fish and crawfish, and, yes, odd to relate, it enjoys making a meal of a skunk. It will take poultry when given the opportunity, but is by and large a beneficial species.

This owl is at home in various habitats, from deep forests to the limit of trees in the north. It also lives in semidesert country and on the open plains.

The Great Horned Owl lays its eggs in old nests of hawks, crows, and eagles, or it may nest on bare ground, on a ledge, or in a tree cavity, in which case it lays its two or three eggs amidst a pile of bones, fur, and feathers.

It has one unusual habit. It mates and lays its eggs especially early, even in the North. As far north as the state of Michigan it is known to lay its eggs in late February, and during very mild winters, even earlier. It is quite a strange sight to see a big mother Horned

Owl setting on her eggs with a cover of snow on her back.

In general the plumage of the adult is brown above, mottled with white, and with a white neck collar. Below, the adult is whitish, narrowly barred with brown. The toes are completely feathered. The eyes are yellow, the beak black. In some areas of the West the plumage is pale in color, and in the Far North, paler still.

The young are heavily barred with black.

The Great Horned Owl is found over much of North America from Alaska south through Mexico, and again southward to the Strait of Magellan in South America.

SNOWY OWL, GREAT WHITE OWL, or ARCTIC OWL: Nyctea scandiaca

This large, powerfully built white owl has a big round head. It looks like a northern bird and it is—an Arctic species living on the Arctic tundra and in swamps and open areas in the Far North. Its feet are so heavily covered with down feathers—the feathers even covering most of the black claws—that the bird looks as if it were wearing fur boots. And its black bill is also nearly hidden by feathers. It is twenty-four inches in length and has a great wingspread of sixty inches. There are no ear tufts.

Not only is this owl conspicuous in size and color,

97

Snowy Owl

but, unlike most owls, it flies in the daytime. Of course a Snowy Owl of the Far North is forced to hunt by daylight during the summer months when the sun never sets.

Snowy Owls are ground-nesting birds, which is as might be expected since quite a large area of their home territory is beyond the limit of trees. They line their nests with grasses and feathers. They generally lay from five to seven eggs.

The main foods of the Snowy Owl are lemmings, mice, and northern hares. They also take rabbits, ground squirrels, shrews and moles, and some birds; when this food is scarce, they eat fish and carrion.

The big yellow eyes are set in a face that is not as flat as the faces of most owls. The plumage of the adult male may be pure white, though the plumage of the upperparts is usually broken here and there with bars of burnt umber or gray-brown. The adult female is heavily barred with burnt umber and gray-brown, both above and below, except for the face, throat, and upper breast. The juveniles are gray all over, while the immature birds are much more heavily barred than their parents.

The Snowy Owl breeds from well within the Arctic Circle into northern Canada and usually winters, too, within this territory. However, in cycles of about four or five years, or sometimes longer periods, lemmings and hares become scarce in the Far North. Then the Snowy Owls migrate southward, looking for food, and we have a chance to see these great white owls within the borders of our northern states. During some of these cycles, Snowy Owls have been reported even as far south as Georgia and South Carolina, Louisiana, Texas, and California. In other years only a few wander southward.

HAWK OWL: *Surnia ulula*

The Hawk Owl is so named because it not only looks hawk-like but flies in some ways more like a hawk than an owl. Also, it is quite active by day.

The head of this owl is quite pointed, rather than very round like most owls, and its tail is very long for an owl. Much bigger, say, than the tiny Saw-whet Owl, it is still a rather small owl with an overall length of seventeen inches and a wingspread of thirty-four inches. There are no ear tufts.

Its flight is as noiseless as other owls but it hunts in much the same way as a Sparrow Hawk does. It flies swiftly and usually low over the ground, flapping, gliding, then hovering. It feeds mostly on lemmings, mice, and other small mammals, and will take some insects and some birds.

Hawk Owl

It is a bird of the northern forests, an Arctic species, and diurnal in habits. It lives in the open bushy country and the open woods.

The Hawk Owls nest in natural cavities in trees or in old woodpecker holes or in abandoned crow and hawk nests and sometimes on stumps. There are three to seven eggs.

The Hawk Owl looks as though it were wearing little boots to keep itself warm in the Arctic cold. The legs are heavily feathered right down to the talons. In the adult plumage the upperparts are brown, barred, and spotted with white. The underparts are white and heavily barred with brown. The facial disc is gray-white with a brown ruff. The beak and eyes are yellow. The plumage of the young is not as dark as that of the adults.

The Hawk Owl breeds as far north as the limit of trees, south into Canada, and comes into the northern United States only as a rare winter migrant. Like the Snowy Owl, it may suddenly appear more numerous south of its breeding range, forced to migrate no doubt by a shortage of mice and other prey in its home territory.

PYGMY OWL: *Glaucidium gnoma*

This tiny owl with big feet for its size is about as large as a Fox Sparrow. It has a length of six and a half inches and a wingspread of fifteen inches. Its legs and feet are feathered. It has a long tail. Its head is small and round. There are no ear tufts.

Pygmy Owls hunt mostly at dawn and twilight but are also active in broad daylight and after dark. Its flight, most unusual for an owl, is rather uneven and, unlike all other owls, it is not silent. The wings make a

Pygmy Owl

whistling sound, like those of the Mourning Dove. The bird also has the unusual habit of flicking its tail.

The Pygmy Owl preys on insects but also makes good use of its oversize feet to catch birds, mice, young squirrels and other rodents, some of which are bigger than itself. It nests in abandoned woodpecker holes or in hollow stumps. The female lays three to four eggs.

There are two color phases of Pygmy Owls. The grayish-brown phase is gray-brown above with buff spots on the back and white spots on the tail. The face, eyebrows, and collar are white. The plumage below is white streaked with dark brown. The rufous phase is rufous brown above with cinnamon spots and white below with rufous streaks. The tail is barred with dark brown. The beak and eyes are yellow, the toes and tarsus—the lower part of the leg—are yellowish.

The young are very much like the adult in coloring.

This is definitely a bird of western North America, ranging from southeastern Alaska and British Columbia down through the Rocky Mountain area to Baja California and into Mexico.

The Ferruginous Owl (*Glaucidium brasilianum*) is an uncommon little owl closely related to the Pygmy Owl and about the same size. In the red (ferruginous) phase, the upperparts are rust-colored and spotted and streaked with buff. The white underparts are streaked with rust color and the tail is barred with brown. There is also a browner phase in which the upperparts are olive brown spotted with white. There are two black patches on the neck, and the face, eyebrows, and collar are white. The underparts are white streaked with olive brown.

The Ferruginous Owl is resident in the lower Rio Grande Valley and Arizona and Texas south into Mexico.

ELF OWL: *Micrathene whitneyi*

This little, elfish-looking owl is the smallest owl in North America. It has a length of only five and a half to six inches and a wingspread of fifteen inches. It has no ear tufts. The bird may be distinguished from the slightly larger Pygmy Owl by its very short tail.

Also, unlike its cousin the Pygmy, the Elf Owl is almost entirely nocturnal in habits.

The Elf Owl is a desert species. It lives in desert and semiarid country and is very common where the Saguaro cacti grow. Many Elf Owls nest high up in these giant cacti in abandoned woodpecker holes. They may also nest in holes in oak, cottonwood, and other trees that grow in the same area as the giant cactus and in trees in the mountains above the desert.

The Elf Owl feeds almost entirely on insects.

There are two color phases, the gray and the brown. The plumage of the adult in the gray phase is brown-gray above, spotted with yellow. The eyebrows and the broken narrow collar are white. The face is cinnamon color. The underparts are white mottled with brown. The brown phase is much the same in markings but deeper brown in color. The eyes are yellow, the beak brown.

The young are similar to the adult.

The Elf Owl breeds from the lower Colorado River Valley of California and Arizona into New Mexico and southwestern Texas.

Most Elf Owls winter south of the United States border.

Elf Owl

BURROWING OWL: *Speotyto cunicularia*

This long-legged, short-tailed, round-headed, horn-less little owl is often found living in abandoned prairie-dog holes. In Florida it may take over an old gopher hole, or it may dig its own burrow in sandy areas. It may be seen on the mound of earth at the burrow entrance, bobbing up and down in a ludicrous way.

The length of this little owl is about nine inches. It has a wingspread of twenty-two inches.

The Burrowing Owl is active by day as well as by night. It feeds on insects, young prairie dogs, ground squirrels, mice and rats, small snakes and other small reptiles, frogs, toads, and small birds.

There are usually six to nine eggs, and both the male and the female share in the incubation.

The Burrowing Owl is now a quite rare species. Men have reduced their numbers by shooting. Also many Burrowing Owls have been killed by ranchers who set out poison bait to get rid of prairie dogs and ground squirrels.

This is a little brown owl. The adult plumage is brown above with whitish spots and white barred with brown below. There is a white stripe over each eye, and the chin is white, separated from the white of the upper chest by a brown band.

The eyes are yellow, the beak dull light yellow or gray.

Burrowing Owl

The young are plain brown above. The underparts are buff with brown on the throat and the sides of the chest.

The breeding range of the Burrowing Owl is on the plains and in open areas from southern British Columbia east to southern Manitoba, south through our western states to Baja California, and eastward to the eastern border of the Great Plains. This owl also lives in Louisiana, Mississippi, and Florida.

The birds winter within much of their breeding range, except for those living in the North, which migrate south to Louisiana, Mississippi, and Florida and as far as southern Mexico.

BARRED OWL or HOOT OWL: *Strix varia*

Somewhat smaller than the Great Horned Owl, the Barred Owl is still a big stout bird. The length is twenty inches and the wingspread is forty-four inches. The bird's head is large and round and has no ear tufts. Its hoot is deep and loud and emphatic, and is usually in eight *whoo whoos,* with a characteristic slurred last note, sounding something like "haw." When two or three males call back and forth to each other the woods resound. However, except for its big voice, the manner of this owl is mild when compared with the Great Horned Tiger of the Air.

The Barred Owl nests early, in March or April, in a hollow tree or in an abandoned nest of a hawk or crow. The female lays two to four eggs.

This owl feeds mostly on mice and other small mammals, but also eats frogs, crawfish and lizards, insects and spiders, and sometimes catches its small relative, the Screech Owl.

As its name indicates, this owl is conspicuously barred. The upperparts are brown barred with white. The rather long tail is crossed by light bars. The wide facial disc is whitish with thin circular bars of brown and generally bordered with a brown ruff. The breast is barred, too, but the belly is heavily streaked, up and down, with brown.

The eyes are luminous and very dark. This bird and the Barn Owl are the only owls that do not have yellow eyes. The yellowish toes are almost completely feathered. The claws are dull yellow-gray and the bill is yellowish.

The young are more broadly barred, and the underparts completely barred.

The Barred Owl likes solitude and lives mostly in the thick growth of swampy woodlands. In this habitat, its hoot is heard over northern Canada south into the United States east of the Rocky Mountains and south again into Mexico and Central America.

Barred Owl

Spotted Owl

SPOTTED OWL: *Strix occidentalis*

The Spotted Owl, often called the western Barred Owl, is just that—a western Barred Owl, completely barred on its underparts and white spotted above. It is a little smaller than the eastern Barred Owl.

This uncommon species lives in the forests of the Pacific coastal area from southwestern British Columbia south to California and in the Rocky Mountains through the southwestern states into Mexico.

GREAT GRAY OWL: *Strix nebulosa*

This big, long-tailed owl is thirty inches in length and has a wingspread of sixty inches. It looks even larger than it is because its plumage is thick and fluffy. It has no ear tufts.

It is mainly a bird of the North, and so it is partly diurnal. It is more nocturnal farther south.

The Great Gray Owl builds a nest of sticks, lined with pine needles, feathers, or bark or hair, in a tall tree. There are two to four eggs. It feeds on mice and squirrels, hares and rabbits and birds.

Notable are the concentric gray circles on the facial disc. The general color above, including the tail, is gray-brown mottled with white. Below, the bird is gray-white, streaked on the breast and streaked and barred on the belly with brown. This owl is feathered to the toes and its small eyes are yellow.

Great Gray Owl

The young are darker, with more bars all over and white spots above.

The breeding range of this big owl is from the limit of trees in Alaska and Mackenzie south into the northwestern United States and east to Ontario and Quebec and Minnesota.

In the winter most Great Gray Owls stay within their breeding range but an occasional one sometimes strays southward.

LONG-EARED OWL: *Asio otus*

This is a medium-sized owl, about halfway between the Great Horned Owl and the Screech Owl. It is not as heavyset as most owls, and is distinguished by its long ear tufts that are set conspicuously closer together than those of the Great Horned Owl. The facial disc forms a prominent V in the center, giving the bird a distinctive appearance and making the head look slightly egg-shaped.

The wingspread of the Long-eared Owl is forty inches and its length is sixteen inches.

The Long-eared Owl is a beneficial species, feeding mostly on mice and other small mammals and taking a few birds. It hunts entirely at night on silent wings. In flight the ear tufts are laid flat against the head.

In the daytime it usually sleeps among the dense

Long-eared Owl

foliage of an evergreen tree, rather than in hollow tree trunks and other cavities as most owls do.

It nests usually in a dense evergreen tree, ten to forty feet above the ground, although it sometimes remakes old nests of crows, squirrels, or hawks. The nest is loosely constructed of sticks and lined with weeds and leaves. The eggs usually number four or five.

The color of the adult is dark brown above, mottled with white and buff. The underparts are white and buff streaked and barred in brown. The legs and feet are feathered to the black claws. The tail is barred and mottled. The facial disc is black around the eyes fading to light tan, and the ruff is speckled. The beak is black, the eyes yellow.

The young are broadly barred, except on the belly.

The Long-eared Owl is common from southern Alaska through Canada south to northern Baja California, in our southwestern states, and in the East to Virginia. It winters from southern Canada south to our southern states and Mexico. In winter a number of the owls may roost together in a grove of evergreen trees.

SHORT-EARED OWL: Asio flammeus

The Short-eared Owl is a little smaller—fourteen inches in length—than the Long-eared, but has a slightly larger wingspread—forty-two inches. The short ear tufts are very inconspicuous.

It is one of the few owls to fly before nightfall. It is active at dawn and dusk, and by day during stormy weather, but also hunts at night. In the Far North, however, where the sun never sets all summer long, the Short-eared Owl, like the Snowy Owl and others that live in the Arctic, has to hunt exclusively by daylight.

The Short-eared Owl is a very beneficial species, feeding mostly on mice and other small rodents and taking a few birds, some insects, frogs, and small snakes. This owl has very big ear openings, and scientists believe that when it flies low over open country in pursuit of mice, the bird hears, rather than sees, its prey.

Short-eared Owl

While most birds of prey do not live in flocks, the Short-eared Owls often nest in colonies, each pair making its nest on the ground in a meadow or marshland. The female lays from two to four eggs.

The plumage of the adult is a mixture of yellow-white and brown stripes, with tail and wings barred. The light yellow eyes are usually circled with rings of dark brown feathers. The rest of the facial disc is dark tan. There is a small black patch on the turn of the underwing. The talons and beak are black. The legs and toes have short feathers.

The upperparts of the young are darker than those of the adult and plain ochre beneath.

The Short-eared Owl is found in open country, breeding from the Arctic Ocean south through Canada to Virginia in the East and to California, Utah, Colorado, Kansas, Missouri, Illinois, and Ohio.

It sometimes winters within its breeding range but more often from British Columbia south in the United States to Baja California, Texas, and the Gulf states, including Florida.

BOREAL OWL: *Aegolius funereus*

This small, chunky northern owl has a short tail and is feathered to its toes. It is a little bigger than the Saw-whet, to which it is closely related. It has a length

Boreal Owl

of twelve inches and a wingspread of twenty-four inches. It has no ear tufts.

The Boreal Owls are partly diurnal in the North. Farther south they are nocturnal.

Like the Saw-whet Owls, the Boreal Owls feed mostly on mice and other small mammals and small birds. They also take bats and sometimes insects. They nest in cavities in trees, often old woodpecker holes, and there are usually five or six eggs.

The plumage of the adult is light brown spotted with white. The collar is white. The facial disc is white, too, bordered with dark brown. Below, the plumage is white with light brown streaking. The eyes and beak are yellow.

The young are all brown, except for a few white spots.

The breeding range of the Boreal Owl is from northern Alaska and northern Yukon and Mackenzie south through the Canadian provinces to northern British Columbia and eastward to the Gulf of St. Lawrence.

Some winter within the breeding range. Other Boreal Owls migrate south to the northern states, sometimes as far south as Nebraska and Illinois, and in the East, rarely, to Massachusetts, Connecticut, Rhode Island, New York, and Pennsylvania.

SAW-WHET OWL: *Aegolius acadicus*

This small owl has a chunky body, a very large head, a large facial disc, and a very short tail. Eight inches long, it is a little smaller than the Boreal. The wings, however, are quite wide, with a spread of eighteen inches. The toes on its big feet are almost completely feathered. It has no ear tufts.

This owl is named for its peculiar cry, heard most often during the early spring and resembling somewhat

Saw-whet Owl

the sound of a saw being filed. The bird also monotonously whistles *too, too, too.*

The Saw-whet spends the daylight hours hiding in trees or in thick foliage of trees. It nests in hollows in trees and stumps or in old woodpecker holes. There are usually three to six eggs.

It is a beneficial species, feeding mostly on mice, shrews, rats, and squirrels. It will also take some small birds and sometimes insects.

The adult Saw-whet is brown above, mottled with white. Below, it is white streaked with brown. The tail is barred with white. The facial disc is pale tan streaked with brown, and the eyebrows are white. The young are plain brown above, their underparts light brown and buff.

The Saw-whet breeds from southern Alaska and Canada south to the mountains of West Virginia, Maryland, Oklahoma, Missouri, Ohio, and Arizona, and on the west coast to the mountains of California. It winters within its breeding range or farther south in our southern states, including Florida.

PROTECTION OF
BIRDS OF PREY

As we have pointed out, almost all species of birds of prey are becoming scarce where they used to be numerous. Some, such as the Osprey, have decreased alarmingly. The Peregrine Falcon is gone from parts of its former range. The California Condor, the Everglade Kite, and the southern Bald Eagle are rare and are in danger of becoming extinct.

In the text we have noted how each endangered species is being protected by laws against shooting, by the setting aside of sanctuaries, by the education of the public to acquaint them with the problems, and by research on the part of scientists and conservationists into how best to increase the population of these birds.

The sanctuaries that afford protection for birds of prey as well as other wildlife, both bird and mammal, are now numerous. So are the research centers. We want here to give a brief mention of one sanctuary and one research center, which are only samples, but good ones.

A UNIQUE SANCTUARY: *Hawk Mountain*

Not too many years ago people considered hawks to be "vermin," pests to man. The average farmer believed that every hawk was a potential chicken killer. Even if he knew that many hawks preyed mostly on his real enemies, rodents and rabbits, the farmer could not tell one hawk from another, and he shot any hawk that came within the range of his gun.

Thousands of hunters agreed with the farmers. They thought that all hawks were killers of game birds. They hunted hawks, not for game to be eaten, but for the "sport" of marksmanship. During the fall migrations, when hawks and other birds of prey, including eagles, Ospreys, vultures, and Peregrine Falcons were winging their way southward, the hunters would go up into the mountains over which the birds passed and shoot them.

In 1929, the game commission of Pennsylvania supported legislation placing a five-dollar bounty on the Goshawk, one of the worst chicken and game-bird hawks. Goshawks are not common in Pennsylvania, but the bounty on them further stimulated hunters in that state to get all hawks, the very beneficial species as well as the Goshawks.

One of the main flyways for the birds of prey in the East led over the Kittatinny ridge, a razorback ridge in Pennsylvania, then known as Blue Mountain. Here, particularly when a northwest wind was blowing, hundreds and hundreds of birds of prey could be seen flying south from September into the late fall. On weekends during the season several hundred hunters would climb to the lookout on Blue Mountain and bring down as many as three hundred birds in a day, all in the name of destroying the enemies of bird and game life.

At that time a few foresighted and educated people were friends of hawks and eagles. In 1934 one of them, Mrs. Charles Noel Edge of New York City, purchased Blue Mountain and founded there what is now known as Hawk Mountain, a unique sanctuary. Although some birds of prey as well as a quantity of other game do live protected there, Hawk Mountain was not designed, as many sanctuaries are, as a home for wildlife. Its prime purpose was to give sanctuary to birds during part of their migratory journey, and there today no guns are allowed. The birds of prey are shot, not by gunmen, but by eager bird watchers with cameras and binoculars.

For the full and exciting story of Hawk Mountain, see the book *Hawks Aloft* by Maurice Broun (Kutztown Publishing Company, Kutztown, Pennsylvania).

PATUXENT WILDLIFE RESEARCH CENTER

Another unique sanctuary, designed specifically to "save from extinction endangered American Wildlife species," was established by the Bureau of Sport Fisheries and Wildlife of the United States Department of the Interior, in 1965, on a 355-acre tract of agricultural land in Laurel, Maryland. The location was chosen because of the mild climate. There most wildlife can be kept out of doors all or most of the year.

The purpose of the center is twofold. Research, including research on pesticides, is carried on to discover the scientific means of restoring endangered species, including birds of prey. And birds and animals are propagated so that they may be released into the wild to restore diminishing populations.

As has been said, the birds of prey that are now in danger of going the way of the Passenger Pigeon and the Dodo bird are the California Condor, the Everglade Kite, the Peregrine Falcon (over part of its range), and the Bald Eagle in the South.

In the case of the California Condor and the Everglade Kite, closely related and common species from South America—the Andean Condor and the South American Snail Kite—are being brought to Patuxent as stand-ins for the North American species for purposes of research.

Any of the endangered birds that are actually bred and raised at the center will be released after no more than one or two generations in the hope that they will not have lost their keen ability to fend for themselves in the wild.

Index

Accipiter cooperii, 32-34
Accipiter gentilis, 27-30
Accipiters, 27-34, 72, 73
Accipiter striatus, 30-32
Accipitridae, family, 18-65
Accipitrinae, subfamily, 26-34
Aegolius acadicus, 121-123
Aegolius funereus, 119-121
American Eagle, 58-62
Aplomado Falcon, 82
Aquila chrysaetos, 55-57
Arctic Owl, 97-100
Asio flammeus, 117-119
Asio otus, 115-117
Audubon's Caracara, 69-71

Bald Eagle, 4, 56, 58-62, 124, 127
Barn Owl, 89-92
Barred Owl, 109-111

beneficial species, 5, 6, 13
   34, 35, 38, 43, 48, 50,
   85, 89, 91, 92, 115, 122
Big Hoot Owl, 94-97
Bird Hawks, 26-34
Black Hawk, 54
Black Vulture, 14-15
Boreal Owl, 119-121
Broad-winged Hawk, 40-42, 72
Broad-winged Rodent
   Hawks, 34-54
Bubo virginianus, 94-97
Burrowing Owl, 107-109
Buteo albicaudatus, 47
Buteo albonotatus, 45-46
Buteo brachyurus, 47
Buteo harlani, 37-38
Buteo jamaicensis, 35-37
Buteo lagopus, 48-50

129

Buteo lineatus, 38-40
Buteo nitidus, 51
Buteo platypterus, 40-42
Buteo regalis, 50-51
Buteo swainsoni, 43-45
Buteogallus anthracinus, 54
Buteoninae, subfamily, 34-62
Buteos, 34-54
Buzzard Hawk, 35-37

California Condor, 1, 4,
    15-17, 124, 127
Caracaras, 69-74
Caracara cheriway, 69-71
Caracara, Common, 69-71
Cathartes aura, 12-14
Cathartidae, family, 12-17
Chicken Hawk, 5, 27-30, 32,
    38
Circinae, subfamily, 63-65
Circus cyaneus, 63-65
classification, 1, 8, 10, 11
color phases, 8
Coragyps atratus, 14-15
Common Caracara, 69-71
Cooper's hawk, 32-34
Crested Caracara, 69-71

diurnal birds of prey, 1,
    11-86
diurnal owls, 99, 100, 102,
    107, 113, 117, 120
Duck Hawk, 79-82

eagles, 55-62, 72
early nesters, 96, 110
eggs, 4

Elf Owl, 105-106
Elaninae, subfamily, 18-20
Elanoides forficatus, 20-22
Elanus leucurus, 18-20
endangered species, 15, 18,
    24, 62, 69, 82, 124, 127
Everglade Kite, 24-26, 124,
    127

Falco columbarius, 82-84
Falco femoralis, 82
Falco mexicanus, 78-79
Falco peregrinus, 72, 79-82,
    124, 127
Falco rusticolus, 75-77
Falco sparverius, 84-86
Falconidae, family, 69-86
Falconiformes, order, 11-86
Falconinae, subfamily, 74-86
falconry, 55, 72-74
falcons, 69, 72-86
Ferruginous Hawk, 50-51
Ferruginous Owl, 104
fish eagle, 59
fish hawk, 65-69
Flammulated Owl, 94
flight, 2, 3, 88
food, 1, 2

Glaucidium brasilianum, 104
Glaucidium gnoma, 102-104
Golden Eagle, 55-57, 72
Goshawk, 27-30, 32, 73, 125
Gray Hawk, 51
Great Gray Owl, 113-114
Great Horned Owl, 94-97
Great White Owl, 97-100

Gymnogyps californianus, 15-17
Gyrfalcon, 72, 75-77

habitat, 3
Haliaeetus leucocephalus, 58-62
Harlan's Hawk, 37-38
harriers, 18, 63-65
Harris' Hawk, 51-54
Hawk Mountain, 125, 126
Hawk Owl, 100-102
hawks, 26-54
Hen Hawk, 27-30, 35-37, 38
Hoot Owl, 109-111

Ictinia misisippiensis, 22-23
identification of birds of prey, 6-8
immature birds, 8
incubation, 4

juvenile birds, 8

Kestrel, 73, 84-86
kites, 18-26

largest bird of prey, 15
Long-eared Owl, 115-117

Marsh Hawk, 63-65
mating, 4
Merlin, 82-84
Micrathene whitneyi, 105-106
migration, 5, 126

Milvinae, subfamily, 18, 22-26
Mississippi Kite, 22-23
Monkey-faced Owl, 89-92

nests, 3, 4, 89
nocturnal birds of prey, 1, 87-123
Nyctea scandiaca, 97-100

Osprey, 65-69, 124
Otus asio, 92-94
    flammeolus, 94
    trichopsis, 94
owls, 1, 87-123

Pandion haliaetus, 65-69
Pandionidae, family, 65-69
Parabuteo unicinctus, 51-54
Patuxent Wildlife Research Center, 127-128
Peregrine Falcon, 72, 79-82, 124, 127
Perninae, subfamily, 18, 20-22
Pigeon Hawk, 82-84
plumage, 6-8
Prairie Falcon, 78-79
Pygmy Owl, 102-104

rare species, 15, 18, 24, 62, 69, 82, 124, 127
Red-shouldered Hawk, 38-40
Red-tailed Hawk, 4, 35-37
Rodent Hawks, 34-54
Rostrhamus sociabilis, 24-26
Rough-legged Hawk, 48-50

sanctuaries, 62, 124-128
Saw-whet Owl, 121-123
scavengers, 12-17, 69-71
Screech Owl, 92-94
Sharp-shinned Hawk, 30-32
Short-eared Owl, 117-119
Short-tailed Hawk, 47
Short-winged Bird Hawks,
    26-34
smallest owl, 105
Snail Kite, 24-26
Snowy Owl, 97-100
Sparrow Hawk, 73, 84-86
Speotyto cunicularia,
    107-109
Spotted Owl, 112-113
Spotted Screech Owl, 94
Strigidae, family, 89, 92-123
Strigiformes, order, 1, 87-123
Strix nebulosa, 113-114
Strix occidentalis, 112-113
Strix varia, 109-111

Surnia ulula, 100-102
Swainson's Hawk, 43-45
Swallow-tailed Kite, 18,
    20-22

Tiger of the Air, 94-97
True Kites, 18, 22-26
Turkey Vulture, 12-14
Tyto alba, 89-92
Tytonidae, family, 89-92

vultures, 11-17

Whiskered Owl, 94
White-tailed Hawk, 47
White-tailed Kite, 18-20
wildlife refuges, 62, 124-128

young birds, 4, 8, 9

Zone-tailed Hawk, 45-46

ABOUT THE AUTHOR AND THE ARTIST

Dorothy Childs Hogner is a Connecticut Yankee born in Manhattan. The daughter of a doctor, she lived the first year of her life in New York. Then her family moved to an old white clapboard house on a hundred-acre farm in Connecticut.

Mrs. Hogner attended Wellesley College in Massachusetts, Parsons School of Design in New York, and was graduated from the University of New Mexico. She is the author of many books for children, nearly all of which are illustrated by her husband, Nils Hogner.

Mr. Hogner is primarily a mural painter. One of his historical murals is in the high school in Litchfield, Connecticut, and his Memorial to the Four Chaplains may be seen at Temple University in Philadelphia.

The Hogners live on an herb farm in Litchfield, Connecticut.